AN INTRODUCTION TO LAW AND LEGAL REASONING

AN INTRODUCTION TO LAW AND LEGAL REASONING

Second Edition

Steven J. Burton
William G. Hammond Professor of Law
University of Iowa

ASPEN LAW & BUSINESS
Aspen Publishers, Inc.

Library of Congress Catalog No. 94-74423

ISBN 0-7355-2594-3

7 8 9 0

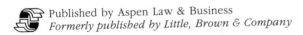 Published by Aspen Law & Business
Formerly published by Little, Brown & Company

Printed in the United States of America

For Jacob Harlan Stier

SUMMARY OF CONTENTS

CONTENTS

PREFACE TO THE SECOND EDITION

IT IS COMMONLY SAID that a beginning law student's first goal is to learn how to "think like a lawyer." For the most part, however, law teachers do not deal explicitly and systematically with legal reasoning. The first-year curriculum in U.S. law schools consists largely of courses on selected basic areas of the law, such as contracts, torts, property, criminal law, and civil procedure. Students read examples of legal reasoning (mostly as expressed in judicial opinions) within the subject of study. Law teachers challenge students to explain and criticize the examples to shed light on the law. Students are left largely to their own devices to extract worthwhile lessons about legal reasoning from the examples and discussions. This book tries to help students learn legal reasoning as it is practiced conventionally in the United States.

This second edition results from a complete rewriting and simplification of the original. I owe debts of gratitude to many people who helped this book reach its present state of maturity. I reaffirm the acknowledgements in the first edition, especially those to Owen Fiss, Serena Stier, Christopher D. Stone, and my father. I add a special thanks to my colleague Ken Kress; many conversations with him over the last decade have helped me to refine my thoughts about legal reasoning. I thank Colleen Halliman, David Jung, Linda Meyer, Serena Stier, and Jill Van Wormer for helpful comments on the manuscript for the second edition. Anne Brafford's extensive editorial comments and suggestions were exceptionally valuable and refreshingly honest. I am grateful as always for the continuing generous support of Dean N. William Hines and the University of Iowa Law School Foundation. Finally, I thank the more than 2,500 students at Iowa who have been through my introductory course on legal reasoning over the last dozen years. Many of them stimulated improvements from the first edition. They provide me the best of reasons for teaching and writing in this area.

AN INTRODUCTION TO LAW AND LEGAL REASONING

Introduction

A LAWYER'S PRINCIPAL TASK, among several, is to help a client get somewhere the client wants to go. To do so, lawyers make predictions and arguments. They attempt to predict what judges (or other adjudicators) will do so their clients can avoid running afoul of the law. They try to convince judges to apply the law favorably in cases involving their clients' interests. Judges, of course, decide what the law permits or requires of people in cases that come before courts.[1]

What is *the law*? Philosophers have debated the question for centuries. For present purposes, let us think of the law as the collection of precedents, rules, principles, and policies employed by judges when justifying their decisions. By all accounts, judges are under a duty to uphold the law. They should apply the law to the facts of a case to yield *legal reasons*, which are reasons for action by law-abiding people. For example, a red light plus a rule requiring motorists to stop at red lights is a legal reason for Mitchell Motorist to stop. It is also a reason for a lawyer to predict that a judge would fine Mitch if he did not stop, a reason for a prosecutor to urge a judge or jury to convict him, and a reason for a judge or jury to do so. *Legal reasoning* is the process of using legal reasons in legal arguments.

Confusion about law and legal reasoning leads to confusion about almost everything else in the study of law. Remarkably, few books introduce law and legal reasoning explicitly and systematically, as does this one. More remarkably, few are directed at beginning law students, who often find it frustrating to learn how to "think like a lawyer." The conventional wisdom is that you learn legal reasoning by doing it. Consequently, students in the first year of law school are left to proceed largely by trial and error.

I have found over nearly two decades of teaching that mastering law and legal reasoning requires patience, persistence, and practice over an extended period of time. A short and direct explanation, however, can help spur the process along and provide

---

[1] On the influence of courts on lawyering activities outside the courthouse, see Chapter 1 §C.

a broad perspective, perhaps reducing accompanying anxiety. A book like this one can call significant features of law and legal reasoning to your attention, draw connections you might otherwise miss, and place law and legal reasoning in a context where they might make better sense. Of course, as with any worthwhile activity, it will remain your responsibility to develop your own approach through hard work over time.

A.   The Rule of Law

A contrast between the ideal and the practice of law and legal reasoning often bedevils beginning law students. The ideal consists of those ways in which lawyers and judges *should* think and communicate their thoughts. The practice consists of those ways in which lawyers and judges *do* think and communicate their thoughts. Few observers claim that the practice conforms to its ideal. The contrast is troubling because there are good reasons for upholding the ideal.

In U.S. society, the ideal reflects a set of values called the "rule of law." Americans believe as a matter of principle that the coercive powers of government should be limited by law. The U.S. Constitution, for example, provides that "[n]o person shall . . . be deprived of life, liberty, or property, without due process of law."[2] Much of what government does, of course, deprives people of life, liberty, or property. A court's judgment may require one person to pay money or transfer property to someone else, may incarcerate a person or otherwise restrict her freedom, or may impose the death penalty. A court may approve or disapprove actions by the police or other officials with similar effects on people. By the most widely accepted accounts, the rule of law requires coercion to be used by officials only when and as authorized by the law.

Accordingly, people want to know by what right someone sitting behind a bench or standing behind a badge uses the state's power to deprive someone else. The law is supposed to provide an answer to that query. Legal reasoning is supposed to draw a connection between the law and a particular action, implementing

---

[2] U.S. Const., amends. V, XIV.

the rule of law. Faulty legal reasoning signifies a faulty connection, raising the question whether governmental power is being used without proper justification.

One version of the rule of law, often called "legal formalism," insists that legal reasoning should determine all specific actions required by the law based only on objective facts, unambiguous rules, and logic. Were the law to operate this way, legal reasoning would lead to the same decision no matter who is doing it. Justice would not vary with the vagaries of human personality. Law and legal reasoning would suffice for lawyers to predict with confidence what government officials will do. Judges could decide cases with no need for judgment. And critics could say with confidence which judicial decisions were lawful.

It takes little exposure to law study to begin doubting whether the practice is anything like the formalist version of the rule of law. Close analysis of many legal decisions shows them to rest on debatable facts, ambiguous laws, or incomplete logic. The "real" grounds of the decision then are unclear. Comparisons of decisions reached by different officials in similar situations may suggest that the officials' personalities, politics, or prejudices had more to do with the decision than did the law. Such a reaction to legal formalism is called "legal skepticism."

Legal skepticism is troubling in two ways. First, how can a genuine skeptic function as an effective lawyer if legal reasoning cannot be relied on to connect law with official action? The law game may seem to go on without rules or with rules that can be changed or ignored at an umpire's whim. Second, why should such a game go on? The law makes some people rich and some people poor, some people free and some people fettered, some people live and some people die—in the real world. A game that does so for no reason or for the wrong reasons is not a game we should want to play in a democratic society committed to freedom and equality.

Consequently, we may confront a legal problem with conflicting instincts. We may try to solve it as required by the formalistic version of the rule of law. At the same time, we may rely on whatever intuitions we have about the nonlegal causes of legal decisions. The implications of each approach differ frequently. We may be confused because it is hard to give up either instinct. We then may not know what we should do.

B.   A Practical Approach

Notice, however, that formalism and skepticism both depend on formalism's view of the law as a matter of rules and logic dictating results in all cases. Formalism holds that law and legal reasoning must satisfy its standard and claims that this standard can be satisfied in practice. Skepticism agrees that law and legal reasoning *must satisfy formalism's standard*, but it claims that, realistically, that standard is not or cannot be satisfied in practice. I suggest that the successful study of law requires a third and more practical approach to legal problems—one that abandons formalism's standard completely.

To lay a basis for this alternative, consider a crucial difference between law and the empirical sciences. In the physical and social sciences, a law is a general description of the regularities in the behavior of persons, events, or things. A descriptive law in principle is falsified by one replicable instance in contradiction to it. The law of gravity, for example, predicts that my pencil will drop to the ground every time I release it (under normal circumstances). If once I released my pencil and it floated to the ceiling, however, this law would come into question. Formalism's standard treats legal laws in a similar way. It requires the rules, facts, and logic to fix lawful conduct in any case; otherwise, the skeptic says, the law is indeterminate and has no effect at all.

Legal laws, however, do not describe regularities in the behavior of anything. Rather, these laws *prescribe* human conduct: They say how people *ought to act*. When Mitch Motorist runs a red light, even repeatedly, whether or not he gets caught, the relevant traffic law does not lose its validity. Mitch is properly cited and fined if and when he gets caught. He violated the law by failing to do what the law prescribes. The law might lose its force if disobedience were persistent and widespread, as when the laws of Eastern European communist regimes were widely flouted in 1989. Occasional violations, however, are simply occasions for officials to apply the law.

Practical choices—those concerning human action—must be made and understood from an actor's point of view, not an observer's. When Mitch encounters a red light, an observer might be stationed on the curbside, recording the correlations between red lights and stopping cars, and observing an apparently causal connection. The observer, like an empirical scientist, is interested in describing the regularities and making predictions of future behavior by motorists. For her, the observations yield *reasons for beliefs*.

Mitch, however, is in the driver's seat. He is uninterested in descriptions of the regularities in motorists' behavior or causal connections between red lights and stopping cars. To Mitch, the red light is not a sign that he will stop. Together with the law, it is a reason for him to stop.[3] Unlike the observer, he has *reasons for action* based in the law. Beliefs stemming from empirical observations, such as the rate at which police detect violations, may supply relevant information to him: Given an impatient character, Mitch might regard a low rate of detections as part of a reason to run the light. A judge and jury can fine him nonetheless for violating the law when he fails to do what the law prescribes.

Whether acting, advising an actor, or judging an actor's conduct, what matters are the reasons indicating what the actor should do. Notice that we can understand the actor's point of view significantly even when we are not in the driver's seat and do not identify with the actor.[4] For example, a Christian may say to his Muslim friend who is about to eat some pork fried rice unwittingly, "You ought not eat that." The Christian thereby speaks from the point of view of one who accepts the Muslim ban on eating pork without endorsing it as right and proper. Similarly, law teachers and practitioners can speak from the point of view of law-abiding citizens or judges and say what the law requires without thereby endorsing it as just and moral. From that point of view, the law will provide reasons for action, as in the example above.

Reasons for action are not subjective. A red light is a reason for Mitch to stop only if it is a reason for *anyone* to stop under the same circumstances. If Mitch were an ambulance driver with siren screaming, the law would allow him to run the red light. So, too, anyone driving an ambulance with a screaming siren could run the red light. Moreover, reasons allowed by the law—legal reasons—may not have the final word on what anyone should do. When Mitch is rushing his seriously ill wife to the hospital at 3:00

---

[3] H.L.A. Hart, The Concept of Law 87-88 (1961).

[4] Joseph Raz, Practical Reason and Norms 171-177 (Princeton Univ. Press ed. 1990).

A.M., he may be morally justified in running a red light even while he is legally liable to pay a fine.

The law may provide competing reasons that must be weighed. When deciding to come to law school, for example, you probably identified the pros and cons, weighed the pros against the cons, and acted according to the stronger reasons in your best judgment. Lawyers and judges often deliberate exactly the same way when engaged in legal reasoning. While you could take into account any reasons you wanted, however, judges are constrained when adjudicating to consider only the reasons allowed by the law.[5] Lawyers take into account a wider range of reasons when predicting official action. Their arguments to judges, however, are limited to the reasons allowed to the judges. Their predictions of judicial behavior are informed centrally by the same reasons.

On this basis, the practice of law and judging can be explained in a practical way that avoids the stark choice between legal formalism and legal skepticism. This approach requires that we consider law and legal reasoning with attention to the point of view of legal actors, including citizens and those who advise and judge them. It also requires that legal reasoning be considered in light of its functions in the real-world contexts in which it is used. In the abstract, legal reasoning does not differ significantly from other kinds of practical reasoning. In real-world settings, it is used by lawyers and judges to deal with distinctively legal problems, is expressed in a specialized language used by a professional community, takes certain principles and goals for granted, and employs artificial devices to circumvent practical problems.

The chief feature of legal reasoning is that it is used in the process of anticipating or settling important disputes in advanced societies. People who live in proximity to one another will find themselves at times in disputes—controversies in which two or more persons claim incompatible rights. Thus, one person may sell another a cow that both had thought was barren. When the cow turns out to be with calf, the seller may try to get the cow back. The buyer may refuse. Or one person may be hunting foxes and begin to chase one. When another person intrudes, and kills and carries off the prey, the first may demand possession of the fox or

---

[5] Steven J. Burton, Judging in Good Faith (1992).

payment of its value. The second may refuse. Or one person may be separating fighting dogs with a stick. When that person carelessly hits another person, the victim may request payment of compensation for an injury. The injurer may refuse. These and countless other situations lead two or more persons to differ over practical matters that will not wait or go away. One person has something the other person claims. Each may refuse to settle the dispute.

Every society develops methods for settling persistent disputes among its members.[6] Different methods are employed by different societies in different times and places. In some, disputes in which the parties persist may be settled by organized combat between the parties (duels), their champions (jousts), or their clans (feuds). They may be settled by ritual appeals for God's judgment (trial by ordeal; consulting an oracle). They may be settled by a third person's command (father knows best; the divine right of kings) or by appeal to chance (flipping a coin). Disputes also may be settled by appealing to a third person's reason, an intellectual search for the fair or right in the matter (arbitration, adjudication).

Important disputes in developed societies can be settled, if need be, by appealing to judges to apply the law. This method is better than the alternatives when disputes should be settled with finality in peaceful and justifiable ways. Dispute settlement by law is more peaceful than duels, jousts, or feuds. It is more just than trial by ordeal, consulting an oracle, flipping coins, or letting a "wise" man decide. And adjudication is more public, accountable, and revisable in cases of error. It seems obvious that law and legal reasoning enable judges to reach final, peaceful, and justifiable dispute settlements better than would the alternatives. What is not obvious is how law and legal reasoning do so.

---

[6] Negotiation, mediation, and conciliation are methods of dispute settlement that may help the disputants settle their differences voluntarily. They do not impose a settlement if the disputants persist. They are increasingly important supplements to adjudication in the U.S. legal system.

C.   Scope

This book is organized into nine chapters. Chapter 1 introduces two basic concepts—cases and rules—from which an understanding of law and legal reasoning should be built. Chapters 2 through 4 introduce and analyze the two main forms of legal reasoning employed by good lawyers and judges. Chapter 2 presents analogical legal reasoning, which is most closely associated with reasoning from precedents. Chapter 3 presents deductive legal reasoning, which is most closely associated with reasoning from rules. Chapter 4 analyzes how analogical and deductive legal reasoning can be combined. These chapters show that these two forms of legal reasoning are useful in several respects and are crucial for expressing the conclusions of legal reasoning effectively. It also shows that, in many cases, they are not adequate to determine legal answers, as required by legal formalism. They leave a judgment of importance unconstrained by the rules and precedents, making it unclear whether legal reasoning can implement the rule of law.

Chapters 5 through 8 supplement precedents and rules with legal principles, policies, and conventions used to make the judgment of importance. Chapter 5 examines the nature of relations among cases and introduces the conventions of the legal community. Chapter 6 introduces the roles of principle and policy. Chapter 7 highlights a judge's perspective on legal reasoning in harder cases. Chapter 8 brings the lessons of preceding chapters to bear on the practical problems of making lawyerly predictions and legal arguments. These chapters show that, though legal reasoning does not produce the certain answers required by legal formalism, it nonetheless produces lawful predictions, arguments, and decisions with a significant degree of regularity. This approach therefore rejects legal skepticism.

Chapter 9, the concluding chapter, responds to a serious objection that might be raised against conventional legal reasoning as presented in the preceding chapters. It addresses the problem of legitimacy in a democratic government under the rule of law—whether the law is compatible with political morality such that it should be obeyed. This book does not conclude that law and legal reasoning achieve legitimacy as currently practiced in the

United States. It suggests, however, the conditions under which a practice like ours could deserve the respect that obedience confers.

Some caveats: This book emphasizes legal reasoning as practiced by lawyers and judges who are worthy of praise by the legal profession. Proceeding this way can be misleading for three reasons. One is that I make judgments to emphasize features I think are important, allowing room for bias to distort the picture. The remedy for this unavoidable problem is not to dismiss what I say due to possible bias or for other superficial reasons. Rather, the remedy is to read the book critically, accepting only those assertions for which convincing reasons are given. Even then, you should believe these lessons only tentatively, pending further thought and experience.

A second risk of misdirection is that the legal system in operation is a good bit messier than the picture I present. Not all lawyers and judges are good at their jobs. (I assume you want to be a *good* lawyer.) The pressures of heavy case loads lead even good lawyers and judges to speak and write in truncated ways. Often the version of legal reasoning presented in this book is only implicit in the practice of law and judging. Sometimes the evidence of practice is too scant to bear any coherent interpretation.

The third, and perhaps most important, caveat is that good legal reasoning is not all there is to good lawyering and judging. The successful practice of law and judging involves ethics, imagination, common sense, and knowledge in the ways of the world, as well as interpersonal, rhetorical, political, and other skills, along with an understanding of the law and proficiency in legal reasoning. A complete theory of lawyering or judging would explain the role of legal reasoning in relation to these other skills; this book suggests only that legal reasoning plays a major role therein.

Upon further study in jurisprudence and legal theory, you would find that much that is said here is controversial among academic theorists. I have chosen to ignore academic controversies except when they bear on matters that should be of concern to beginning law students. Even then, I hope only to identify issues and suggest fruitful avenues of thought. You must do the hard work of spinning a valuable web of beliefs about law for yourself.

CHAPTER ONE

Cases and Rules

MOST LAYPEOPLE probably think of the law as a system of rules, much like the traffic code writ large. The study of law in U.S. law schools, however, normally begins with law cases. You will study primarily from cases throughout law school. Parsing the cases will be an important intellectual activity throughout your legal career. To be sure, legal rules, principles, and policies play an essential role. Cases, however, are the grist for the legal reasoning mill.

Before undertaking the main discussion of legal reasoning, three orienting questions will be posed in this chapter: What is a case? What is a rule? Why do we study primarily cases?

A. Cases

In this book, a *case* is a short story of an incident in which a court acted or may act to settle a dispute. The term is used in other ways for other purposes,[1] but the purpose here is to say something useful about legal reasoning. This definition will help.

Treating a case as a *short story* emphasizes that it has a beginning, a middle, and an end. The story begins when two or more people get into a dispute or one person gets into a dispute with the community as represented by law enforcement officials. In the initial phase, the parties may interact informally or through lawyers. A middle phase commences when one party (the plaintiff or prosecutor) files a complaint against another (the defendant) with a trial court, calling on the court to settle the dispute in favor of the complaining party. It continues in the trial court until a judgment is entered by the presiding judge. If either party believes the judge erred on a point of law, it may appeal to an appellate court, where the last phase takes place. There, arguments are heard by a group of judges who issue a final judgment settling at least

---

[1] For a different perspective, see Owen M. Fiss, The Forms of Justice, 93 Harv. L. Rev. 1, 28-44 (1979).

part of the dispute. The appellate court writes and publishes an opinion that summarizes the facts of the dispute and the proceedings in the trial court, announces a decision on the issues before the appellate court, and gives the reasons for its decision. For the most part, a lawyer's knowledge of decided cases comes from what the appellate courts write in their opinions, which may or may not be accurate stories of the events in question.

Treating a case as a short story of an *incident* emphasizes that every case is unique in all of its particulars. A case involves two or more parties, both of whom are unlikely ever to repeat the very actions that led to the dispute between them. We can describe the events in one case in terms general enough to encompass other disputes between other parties in other times and places. We can also describe them in terms specific enough to encompass only the dispute that occurred between these parties at one time and place. However we describe cases, each occurs once.

Treating a case as a short story of an incident in which *a court acted or may act* emphasizes that we will focus mainly on two sorts of disputes: (1) disputes in the past that were settled, at least in part, by the coercive dispute settlement machinery of the state (decided cases, or "precedents") and (2) unresolved or foreseeable disputes that might be settled in that way (problem cases). A court is a central part of the state's dispute settlement machinery, but only a part. For example, a court's judgment in favor of the plaintiff in a civil case—generally one in which a private plaintiff initiates a lawsuit—may be enforced against a noncompliant defendant by the sheriff. Some of a losing defendant's property may be taken, by force if need be, and sold by the sheriff, with the proceeds going to the plaintiff to pay a money judgment. In criminal cases, the police may initiate the dispute on behalf of the community, and an official prosecutor requests court action. On conviction, a criminal defendant may be fined or incarcerated by the sheriff, using force if necessary. The use of coercion by state officials usually is not necessary because most citizens are law-abiding by disposition and, for others, the threat of force is sufficient to induce compliance. Nonetheless, every request to a court is a request that the state use force, if necessary, to settle the dispute in favor of the complaining party. A court "acts" whether such a request is granted or denied.

Treating a case as a short story of an incident in which a court acted or may act *to settle a dispute* emphasizes the social function of the law. Formal methods of peaceful dispute settlement are needed because disputes will arise whenever people live in close proximity to one another. Some disputes will not be settled by voluntary means. The availability of formal dispute settlement procedures may lessen the level of violence and other disruptions in society by affording the disputants an alternative to fighting. The law courts, by their responses to concrete disputes, also contribute to society's understanding of its values. The law both reflects and helps mold social values, substantially through judicial judgments in cases resolving disputes.

B.   Rules

To explain why we emphasize cases, we should identify the principal alternative—rules. The contrast between cases and rules is not difficult to grasp.

In this book, a *rule* is a general statement of what the law permits or requires of classes of people in classes of circumstances. Again, the term is used in other ways for other purposes. This definition is even more rough than the definition of a case because rules are notoriously slippery characters. Some would draw distinctions between rules and principles or rules and policies, but such distinctions can be deferred to Chapter 6.

Treating a rule as a *general statement* emphasizes that all rules are cast in language. Because all language (save proper names) is general, our words do double- and triple-duty. Consider the word *bar*. You may want to join the bar but may be barred if you fail the bar and wind up tending bar or selling candy bars. A rule that uses the word *bar*, or any other word, requires interpretation to sort out the various possible referents. Legal rules characteristically require interpretation, which is an important part of legal reasoning.

Treating a rule as a general statement *of what the law permits or requires* emphasizes that a rule is normative. That is, a rule guides conduct by saying something about what people in general should or should not do. A rule might include a descriptive part, as when it states the circumstances under which an obligation comes into play. For example, a rule might say that "One who kills another without excuse or justification shall be punished. . . ." The part "One who kills another" purports to describe facts. The part "without excuse or justification" is normative because it requires a judgment of the rightfulness or wrongfulness of a killing. The part "shall be punished . . . " states the legal consequence attaching to unexcused and unjustified killings of people by people. This rule implies an obligation for people not to kill other people wrongfully, though it says little about which killings are wrongful or rightful.

Treating a rule as a general statement of what the law permits or requires of *classes of people in classes of circumstances* emphasizes that rules apply to groups of people in similar situations. Rules operate from a position of generality; that is, they apply to more than one case. Legal rules are supposed to affect what people do by bringing obligation, and often force or the threat of force, to bear on their behavior. Rules consequently should be announced before people engage in relevant behavior and before a case governed by the rule materializes. Because foresight is limited and language imperfect, a rulemaker speaks in generalities. A statement of what the law permits or requires of one person under one set of circumstances—in one case—would be called an *order*.

In sum, a rule stands in contrast to the cases it governs. A rule is a general statement of what the law permits or requires of classes of people in classes of circumstances. A case is a short story of an incident in which a court acted or may act to settle a dispute.

C.   Legal Reasoning and Legal Problems

By the case method of instruction, you will be required in each course to read many opinions in cases decided by appellate courts. In class, you will be asked to describe what the court did in each case, to explain why it did it, to analyze the implications of each case for possible future disputes, and to synthesize the lessons from groups of cases into a general understanding of each topic under study. This process of analyzing and synthesizing cases seeks to develop your capacity to use legal reasoning to solve legal problems. Developing this skill implies a study of what judges do and ought to do—a study of adjudication.

A large part of what lawyers do involves this same skill. But a larger part involves other skills. Much lawyering is an effort to anticipate possible disputes and then to plan a client's activities so that disputes are not likely to arise or can be settled advantageously if they do arise. Much lawyering is an effort to settle existing disputes by negotiation. Indeed, most of the disputes that reach a lawyer are settled before or soon after they reach a court. Most of those that proceed to trial and judgment are not appealed. Lawyers in practice spend the better part of their time planning, counseling, drafting, negotiating, or preparing for trials—anticipating and processing disputes from the law office.

Throughout, however, an important part of lawyering is court-oriented. This part consists of predicting what an appellate court would do if a case were to materialize and be taken to the highest available court, or persuading someone of what an appellate court will or should do in that event. That much more is involved does not mean that predicting and persuading court action are not involved. Some examples illustrate the point while introducing some key functions of a lawyer.

Consider a lawyer who is counsel to a business firm that manufactures and sells a product—say, a chain saw. The seller-client wishes to market a new, improved model. The client seeks legal advice on whether to include a certain kind of chain guard that would reduce the risk of injuries to operators, but only at some increase in the price of the saw (and consequently some reduction in the client's volume of sales and the amount of its profits). The lawyer will want to determine whether omitting the chain guard makes it significantly more likely that the seller will be held liable (that is, will be forced to pay compensation to users of the chain saw for injuries that could have been prevented by a chain guard). The lawyer's prediction of what the law will do in the end—what an appellate court would decide—is a significant element in that determination.

If the lawyer concludes that omitting the chain guard is likely to make no difference before an appellate court, she may advise the client that a decision whether to include a chain guard need not be influenced by legal factors. Further questions will arise if she concludes that omitting the chain guard makes liability more likely: What are the courts likely to do should the seller omit the chain guard but include in the instruction booklet a warning of the danger? Will the courts enforce a contract clause by which the buyers agree to assume the risk of such injuries (a disclaimer of liability)? Will it matter how the language of such a warning or disclaimer is drafted? The lawyer's predictions of judicial action in each variation on the anticipated dispute will influence her advice on whether to include the chain guard. The predictions will also influence her drafting suggestions on language for inclusion in the instruction booklet or contracts of sale.

Assume now that the chain saw is marketed without the chain guard, warnings, or disclaimer. A buyer is injured in a way that would not have occurred with a chain guard. The buyer seeks compensation for his injuries from the seller; the seller does not want to pay. At this point, the seller's lawyer may try to negotiate a favorable settlement while preparing for trial, should a lawsuit be initiated.

The lawyer again will want to predict what a court will do based on the facts then available. The lawyer's advice on whether to settle out of court will be influenced by the prediction in the following way, to give a simplified example.[2] If the buyer claims compensation in the amount of $10,000 and the seller's lawyer predicts that the seller has a 70 percent chance of losing for that amount in court, the lawyer should advise the seller to settle for any amount less than $7,000. The client would be better off settling for less than $7,000 now than taking a 70 percent chance of being forced to pay $10,000 later. On the other hand, if the buyer's lawyer predicts that the buyer has a 40 percent chance of winning in court, the lawyer should advise the buyer to settle for any amount more than $4,000. The client is better off with more than $4,000 for certain than with a 40 percent chance of getting $10,000 later. Given these stakes and these predictions by the two lawyers, the conditions are ripe for settlement somewhere between $4,000 and $7,000.

The lawyers' skills at negotiation will determine the amount of the settlement. Though many factors will influence the negotiation, one will be the lawyers' skills at persuasion. If the seller's lawyer can convince the buyer's lawyer that the probability of a buyer's

---

[2] This example assumes that the people involved are rational and wish neither to gamble nor to avoid risks unreasonably. For purposes of discussion, it also ignores lawyer's fees and other litigation expenses.

victory in court is less than the buyer's lawyer had thought, the buyer's lawyer may advise his client to settle for a lower amount. The converse is also true. The lawyers' persuasive skills may make a settlement possible even if their initial predictions did not set the right conditions. As the lawyering process unfolds, new information is acquired and new arguments are developed. The lawyers should revise their predictions and negotiate further.

Assume now that no settlement was reached and the dispute goes before a trial court. The trial judge will be required to make a large number of decisions, including rulings on pretrial motions, admissibility of evidence, and in some cases instructions to the jury. Each decision affects each party's prospects of winning the lawsuit. These decisions should be made according to the law. If the trial judge errs either by applying the wrong law or, as sometimes happens, by applying the correct law wrongly in the case, the final judgment may be reversed on appeal to a higher court. The lawyers representing the parties will be allowed to make arguments to the trial judge on what the law permits or requires in each decision. These arguments by counsel in large part will seek to persuade the trial judge of what the appellate court would decide on the point if an appeal were taken.

Assume now that the case reaches the highest appellate court in the relevant jurisdiction,[3] the end of the dispute anticipating and processing sequence. The lawyers and the lower court judges wanted to predict what judges further along the sequence would do and persuade others of what those judges would do, to avoid moving to the next stage of the sequence unnecessarily. The highest appellate court does not care to predict what it will itself do. The highest appellate court cares about what it *should* do.

The highest appellate court's concern may be said in general to have two components. First, this court will care that the law be reasonably stable and predictable so that lawyers and lower court judges can do their jobs and people can plan their activities to remain within the law. This will lead the court to give weight to established understandings of what the law *is* because lawyers and lower court judges rely on these understandings. Second, the

---

[3] In some jurisdictions, there are two levels of appellate courts, in which arguments before the intermediate court will focus on persuading the judges of what the highest court would decide.

highest appellate court will care that the law be justified in light of contemporary social, historical, and cultural circumstances and evolving notions of justice. Therefore, the court will be open to arguments that the law should be changed to improve its justification; it will care what the law *ought to be*.

The "is" and "ought" components, however, are not so easily separated in practice. Because the lawyers and lower court judges know that the appellate court may interpret or change the law, their reliance on established law will be incomplete. Their predictions of and arguments about what the highest appellate court would do in the case, like the court's final judgment itself, should be based on the established law and an evaluation of it under contemporary circumstances and in light of evolving notions of justice. Therefore, the lawyers' predictions and legal arguments depend in part on what lawyers think the highest appellate judges will think the law ought to be. The appellate decision depends in part on what the highest appellate judges think lawyers (commonly) think is the law as it stands.

Consequently, decisions of the appellate courts are important throughout the dispute anticipating and processing sequence. From Chapter 2 to Chapter 7, we will emphasize legal reasoning in adjudication, focusing on the law that judges have a duty to uphold. Legal reasoning in counselling and advocacy settings will be reexamined in Chapter 8.

D. Using Rules and Cases

Statements of the law take the form of both rules and cases. To develop skill in legal reasoning, a study of cases is crucial. Rules are deceptively simple in appearance while cases are complex and rich in variety. Sooner or later, you will find that reasoning from rules alone is often unreliable in a world that is more complex and varied than even the cases.

1. Rules in Problem Cases

Using a rule often requires intensive analysis and considerable interpretation. Consider, for example, a simple rule providing that

"No person shall sleep in a city park."[4] Imagine two problem cases.[5] In the first, a gentleman was found sitting upright on a park bench at noon—his chin was resting on his chest, his eyes were closed. The gentleman was snoring audibly. In the second, a disheveled tramp was found lying on the same bench at midnight—a pillow was beneath his head, and a newspaper was spread over his body as a blanket. The tramp, however, had insomnia. Both were arrested under the rule and brought before a court for trial. Would you predict that the gentleman will be convicted and the tramp acquitted? That the gentleman will be acquitted and the tramp convicted? That both will be convicted? That both will be acquitted? Does your answer follow from the language of the rule itself?

Consider, for a second example, a rule providing that "No person shall bring a vehicle into a city park."[6] Imagine some possible problem cases. An ambulance was driven into the park to reach a stricken jogger. The local Jaycees put a World War II tank in the park as a monument to the town's war dead. Some teenagers held a car race, a go-cart race, a bicycle race, or a roller-skating race in the park. A tree surgeon drove his truck into the park to load and remove the branches of a dead tree under contract with the city. Surely some of these incidents would not be violations of the rule. Yet all might be said to involve a person bringing a vehicle into the park. Consequently, merely *saying* in any of these cases that a person brought a vehicle into a park would not be sufficient to persuade someone else *to believe* that the rule had been transgressed.

In almost any case, knowing the rules leaves more intellectual work to be done because rules are expressed imperfectly and projected into an uncertain future. A rule alone does not determine whether many cases come within the class it designates. Whoever states a rule to govern future cases rarely, if ever, will anticipate all of the future situations that might plausibly be described in the

---

[4] This example is adapted from Lon L. Fuller, Positivism and Fidelity to Law: A Reply to Professor Hart, 71 Harv. L. Rev. 630, 662-664 (1958).

[5] The shorthand descriptions of cases may be thought of as "short short stories," which rely on common images to fill in the details.

[6] This example is adapted from H.L.A. Hart, Positivism and the Separation of Law and Morals, 71 Harv. L. Rev. 593, 607 (1958).

language of the rule but that should not be within the class designated by the rule.[7] Consequently, you should analyze and interpret the rules in light of possible cases, using legal reasoning to reach a sound conclusion. Karl Llewelyn overstated the point colorfully in his lectures of 1929-1930 introducing Columbia students to the study of law:

> We have discovered in our teaching of the law that general propositions are empty. We have discovered that students who come eager to learn the rules and who do learn them, *and who learn nothing more*, will take away the shell and not the substance. We have discovered that rules *alone*, mere forms of words, are worthless. We have learned that the concrete instance, the heaping up of concrete instances, the present, vital memory of a multitude of concrete instances, is necessary in order to make any general proposition, be it rule of law or any other, *mean* anything at all. Without the concrete instances the general proposition is baggage, impedimenta, stuff about the feet. It not only does not help. It hinders.[8]

2.   Decided Cases in Problem Cases

Decided cases also can be used in legal reasoning to solve problem cases, with some advantages. Lawyers in practice generally will care less about the law in the abstract than in its practical implications for particular existing or possible future disputes involving a particular client. Judges do not generally enact rules; instead, they decide cases.

Effective legal planning requires a keen sense of the variety of disputes that can arise in the future. A lawyer planning a client's activities is engaged partly in imagining the disputes that might arise from the client's activities and in taking precautions to minimize losses in such disputes. Elegantly drafted contract language may be worthy of praise for its style; it will earn none if a foreseeable dispute arises that was not anticipated in the

---

[7] Consider, also, cases that could not plausibly be described in the language of the rule but that should be within the class.

[8] Karl N. Llewelyn, The Bramble Bush 12 (1951).

drafting. The world has a habit of confounding even those with perspicacious insights and vivid imaginations. A study of the cases stimulates and supplements the imagination so that better precautions can be taken for a greater variety of disputes that might arise from a client's activities.

Once a dispute has arisen, the lawyer will care what a court will or should do *in that case*. Pyrrhic victories, as when a court accepts a lawyer's preferred general rule but concludes that his client loses under that rule, usually are of little interest to the lawyer and even less to the client. To *predict* what the court will do in one case, you can look to what courts have done in other, similar cases. To *persuade* a court of what it should do in one case, you can point out what courts have done in other, similar cases. A practice of comparing and contrasting cases may supply particularities that general rules leave untreated.

Consider again the rule prohibiting any person from bringing a vehicle into a city park. Assume that you are a judge who must decide whether a tree surgeon violated that rule by bringing his truck into the park to load and carry away dead tree branches under contract with the city. You could say that the tree surgeon violated the rule because he is a person, and he brought a vehicle into the park. You could also say that the city, not a "person" within the meaning of the rule, brought the vehicle into the park through its contract with the tree surgeon. The language of the rule allows both interpretations. How should you think your way to a decision?

Assume further, then, that from a previously decided case you know, or from common sense all would agree, that an ambulance can legally enter the park to administer aid to a stricken jogger. Assume also that you know or we can agree that teenagers violate the rule by racing cars in the park. Now you can ask: Is the tree surgeon's truck case more like the ambulance case or more like the racing case?

It would seem that you can reach a reasoned answer to the question, though the reasons do not line up to yield that answer as numbers line up to yield a sum. The ambulance case tells you that the statute should not be interpreted literally, as prohibiting all persons from bringing any vehicle into any city park under any circumstances. There is room for interpretation. The racing case tells you, by inference in light of common sense, that the rule seeks to protect the park and those who seek rest and recreation in the park from noisy and dangerous activities involving vehicles. You might think that, like the rule, the city and the tree surgeon were maintaining the park for the benefit of people who use it. The short intrusion on the tranquillity of the park is small in relation to the benefits. It would be absurd in this day to require the tree surgeon to carry the tree branches out of the park by manual labor or horse-drawn cart (if that is not a "vehicle"!). Therefore, you may conclude, the tree surgeon should not be punished under the rule as properly interpreted.

From a different perspective, a further reason can be given for emphasizing the study of cases: The action of a court to settle a dispute—the decision in a law case—is coercive action by the state involving at least the threatened use of physical force. The law that determines when that power may be used—when the sheriff may deprive an individual of liberty or property pursuant to judicial decree—also determines the limits of our freedom from a major form of state compulsion. The law at the same time partly defines permissible uses of force by the state and the scope of individual liberty. It seeks to rule out arbitrary and oppressive uses of power by the state while allowing justifiable uses of that power. Lawyers are society's experts on when (in what cases) the state may use its coercive powers within the rule of law.

Cases, much more than rules, press us to think hard about justice, the limits of proper governmental power, and the scope of individual freedom. It is easy, for example, to agree on a general rule that promises should be kept. But should a court enforce your promise to pay me $500 for the Eiffel Tower, should you decide not to honor it? Would it make a difference if the Eiffel Tower in mind were a stage prop I had delivered to you for use in a play? Again, should a court enforce your promise to join me for dinner at my club, should you decide not to keep it? Would it make a difference if I had paid you to give an after-dinner speech or that my club discriminates against women? What, exactly, should it mean to "enforce" that promise when the dinner is history?

Cases display the complexities with which the law should deal. Comparing and contrasting cases supplies the particularities needed for lawyers to predict intelligently what a court will do or persuade a court of what it should do in a case, and for judges to make reasoned decisions in problem cases. Comparing and contrasting cases requires hard, rigorous thinking about justice and the proper role of government in a democratic society. Let us turn, then, to the principal form of legal reasoning from cases—the analogy.

CHAPTER TWO _____

Analogical Legal Reasoning

LEGAL REASONING TAKES two principal forms: One is analogical; the other is deductive. These forms perform important practical functions; some means of organizing the mass of legal materials is essential. They can help you to identify the proper starting points for reasoning, locate the relevant materials, and formulate issues to focus deliberation. You will find that poorly formed legal arguments are easily dismissed because they are hard to understand. Chapters 2 and 3 will introduce these forms, beginning with analogies.

The forms of legal reasoning, however, cannot guarantee the soundness of a legal argument. Many well-formed arguments are wrong, while others are less persuasive than competing well-formed arguments. A form is like an empty vessel: Its usefulness resides in the space where there is nothing. As a vessel can carry wine or water, a form can carry sense or nonsense. The soundness of a legal argument depends on how the forms of legal reasoning are filled in—on the content of the statements in an *argument*.

A.   The Analogical Form

Most legal problems in the United States are governed by either the common law or the law enacted by a legislature or an administrative agency. The common law is the law made by judges through their decisions in cases within their authority. Common law making is on a case-by-case basis. The law of contracts, torts, and property is largely common law.

The central tenet of the common law is the principle of *stare decisis*: Points of law once decided in an appropriate case should not be reopened in other cases involving the same point in the same jurisdiction (unless something has changed that justifies changing the law). Accordingly, decided points of law are normally *binding* or *authoritative* and are referred to as *legal authority.* The principle of stare decisis supports the common law doctrine of precedent, which treats previously decided cases as authorities for the decision of later cases. Reasoning under the doctrine of precedent is mainly by analogy, which requires basically that like cases be decided alike.[1] This is a requirement of formal justice.

Analogical reasoning is familiar in everyday nonlegal situations. For example, Mother may allow Older Brother to stay up until 9:00 P.M., and Younger Brother may demand the same treatment. Younger Brother may make an argument for his view by claiming he is like Older Brother because both are children. Therefore, he thinks, they should be treated alike. When Mother rejects his claim, explaining that older children need less sleep than younger children, she is arguing that there is an important difference between her two children. Therefore, she thinks, they should not be treated alike. On reflection, you can imagine any number of familiar situations in which people argue by analogy.

To make any analogical argument, you should take three steps. First, you identify a *base point* situation from which to reason (e.g., Older Brother's bedtime). The base point consists of the relevant facts together with a decision about what someone should do. Second, you describe those factual respects in which the base point situation and the problem situation (Younger Brother's bedtime) are *similar* or analogous (childhood status) and *different* or disanalogous (age). Third, you judge whether the factual similarities or the differences are more *important* under the circumstances. Thus, if childhood status is more important than age in the example, the analogy suggests that Younger Brother's bedtime should also be 9:00 P.M. If age is more important, however, the disanalogy suggests that an earlier time would be justified.

The second and third steps are made necessary by the simple logic of analogies. No two people, acts, or things are alike in all respects. The claim that two people, acts, or things are *alike* is not a claim that they are *identical*. If identical, they would not be two and could not be compared and contrasted at all. Nor will any two people, acts, or things ever be different in all factual respects. If different in all respects, they could not both be people, acts, or

---

[1] On common law rules, see Chapter 4 §A.

things; comparing or contrasting them would be pointless. Therefore, analogical reasoning requires careful consideration of both the similarities and the differences between two situations. The crucial point is judging whether the similarities or differences are more important.

Analogical reasoning is highly dependent on context. It is silly to ask whether Older Brother and Younger Brother are alike or unalike in the abstract: They are both. Significant likeness or unlikeness makes sense only in a concrete setting, as when bedtime is disputed. Even then, likeness or unlikeness may change with the circumstances. Given the fact of a three-year difference in age, for example, the two brothers may be unalike for purposes of bedtime at ages 3 and 6 but alike for the same purposes some years later. And they may be different for purposes of bedtime while similar for purposes of distributing Christmas presents fairly. (This dependence on context is one reason why it is hard to formulate rules that can be applied formalistically without producing some absurd results.)

In most familiar nonlegal settings, analogical reasoning is highly informal. The individuals involved decide what will count as a base point, or an important similarity or difference, for whatever reasons they find appealing. Rarely are they quite aware that they are reasoning "by analogy" or are analyzing (1) the propriety of a base point, (2) the factual similarities and differences between two situations, and (3) the relative importance of the similarities and differences under the circumstances.

B.   Analogical Legal Reasoning

Analogical legal reasoning is not fundamentally different from analogical reasoning in familiar situations. It is, however, more formal, rigorous, and uniform in expression. What can count as a base point or an important factual similarity or difference is constrained by the law, in principle if not always in practice. Underlying good legal reasoning of this kind are well-accepted rules identifying the authoritative base points, a vocabulary and method encouraging rigorous consideration of both similarities and differences, and a form of expression for framing the issue to be decided. Strict analogies, however, leave the crucial judgment of importance—determining whether the factual similarities or differences should control the outcome—unconstrained by the law and open to abuse.

1.   Precedents

The first step in analogical reasoning is identifying a proper base point. In law, the *doctrine of precedent* gives a special status as base points to law cases decided in the past by the highest court in the relevant jurisdiction.[2] The U.S. legal system includes a federal jurisdiction in which federal courts are primarily responsible for matters of national interest. The U.S. Supreme Court is the highest court for these matters. It also includes fifty state jurisdictions in which state courts carry primary responsibility for most other matters. Each state has a highest court, usually called the supreme court of the state.[3] The cases decided in the past by these courts are the most authoritative precedents for deciding future cases within the respective jurisdictions.

Other cases, though of less significance, can serve as persuasive base points. You can use the precedents of any court (including foreign courts) as base points for analogical argument before any other court. If the case is not a binding precedent, it nonetheless may be a well-reasoned decision that a court will find convincing. You also can use hypothetical cases found in the scholarly literature or the American Law Institute's Restatements of the Law, and hypotheticals of your own construction when the result is obvious to reasonable people.

This explanation of the base points in common law adjudication simplifies the rules of the game. For example, it is open to the highest court in a problem case to *overrule* its own precedents. The case that overrules then supplants the case that was overruled as the authoritative base point for future cases of that kind, making a change in the law. Overruling is not a common occurrence,

---

[2] *Jurisdiction* refers to the scope of a court's authority to decide cases lawfully. It may be described in territorial, citizenship, functional, or other terms. Jurisdiction is normally established by the statute creating the relevant court.

[3] In New York, the highest court is called the Court of Appeals, while the trial and intermediate appellate courts are called the supreme courts.

though the possibility is ever-present. Moreover, the complex relationships among courts are treated in specialized law school courses in far greater detail than would be appropriate in this introduction. Here, you only need understand that legal reasoning proceeds on the basis of formal rules that identify authoritative base points for analogical legal reasoning.

2.   *Factual Similarities and Differences*

The second step in analogical reasoning is identifying factual similarities and differences between the base point situation and a problem situation. Legal reasoning by analogy uses a vocabulary and rhetoric that emphasize the need for rigorous attention to both relationships. In controversial cases, which are the problem cases that require lawyerly skill, there will be many precedents that are somewhat similar to the problem case but seem to cut both ways. You should, by rigorous analysis of the facts of the cases, proceed to identify the many plausible points of factual similarity and difference. You can make a good judgment whether the similarities or differences are more important only after you have identified all plausible points of comparison and contrast.

We say that a judge or decision *follows precedent* when the facts of a precedent are so similar to those of a problem case that the same outcome is required (unless the earlier case is overruled). A judge or case *distinguishes precedent* when the facts of a precedent are so different that a different outcome is required. There is no reason to presume in advance of rigorous analysis that a superficially similar precedent should be followed or distinguished. The idea that like cases should be decided alike implies that unalike cases should be decided unalike if the differences are more important under the circumstances. Stare decisis requires judges to distinguish dissimilar precedents as much as it requires them to follow similar precedents.

In principle, then, the doctrine of precedent requires a judge to treat each relevant authoritative precedent in one of three ways: A judge may follow a precedent, distinguish it, or (if on a high enough court) overrule it. A judge may not in good conscience ignore a relevant authoritative precedent, though this sometimes happens and becomes a reason for criticizing the judge. In their arguments, lawyers similarly should advocate that each relevant authoritative precedent be followed, distinguished, or overruled. Legal arguments are seriously vulnerable if they ignore a relevant and unwelcome authoritative precedent. A lawyer who knowingly fails to disclose such a precedent can be subject to discipline by the bar.[4]

Whether a precedent should be followed or distinguished depends in part on a careful analysis of the facts of the precedent in relation to the facts of a problem case. The *facts* of a case consist of a description of the events in the world that set the stage for the dispute, how the parties came to find themselves in dispute, and sometimes what the parties did to try to resolve the dispute on their own. These are all events that normally occur before a court is asked to settle the dispute and mostly can be described in ordinary, nontechnical language. The facts of a case also include a description of the legal proceedings in the lower courts, if any, as necessary to identify the legal point that was or may be appealed to the higher court. Most important, the *legal issue* on appeal always involves the question whether the trial judge erred in making some particular decision under the factual circumstances in the case. The facts and legal issue establish the context in which we make the judgment of importance at the third step.

When working by analogy, you should compile the facts of the problem case as they have been or may be proved in court. Analyze them until you understand them in great detail. Mastery of the legally provable facts is crucial. The presence or absence of a particular fact may become the point on which a precedent is determined to be alike or unalike in an important respect. At the early stages of legal analysis, you never know which facts will matter. Good lawyers err on the side of compiling more facts in greater detail than they are likely to need in the course of legal proceedings.

Then you should locate (by legal research) the facially similar precedents and analyze their facts. Here again, a masterful understanding of the facts is needed, though the facts as summarized in judicial opinions normally are sufficient for this purpose.

---

[4] Model Rules of Professional Conduct Rule 3.3(a)(3) (1992).

You do not yet know which facts will or should matter when a court decides to follow or distinguish each precedent. A good judge will want to hear about all plausible similarities and differences before deciding which are more important under the circumstances.

Only then can you list the factual similarities and differences between each precedent and your problem case. Doing so, of course, is not a mechanical matter of finding identical statements in the descriptions of the cases. You may summarize the facts in your own language. This allows room for insight into relationships among the facts that overly technical or thoughtless descriptions sometimes mask. It also allows room for distorting the facts, though opposing counsel and the judges can be expected to expose such distortions.[5]

3.   The Judgment of Importance

The third step for analogical reasoning is determining whether the factual similarities or the differences between the two situations are more important under the circumstances. In law, the analogical form requires a judgment whether precedents should be followed or distinguished (assuming away any question of overruling). Unlike a layperson, however, a judge in a law case is not free to assign importance for any reason whatever. A judge's duty is to decide that question *according to the law*. But it is most difficult to give a satisfactory account of what this might mean in common law adjudication.

You might think that judging according to the law means following the common law rules at this third step and, therefore, departing from the analogical form of legal reasoning. Common law rules are rules announced by judges in their opinions in cases governed by the common law. These rules, you might think, should perform two functions: They should identify the legally important facts in advance of a case and the required legal consequences when the important facts are presented. For example, a common law rule might provide, "Whenever a man dies without

---

[5] An advocate has an ethical duty of candor when before a court. Id. Rule 3.3.

a will, his property shall become the property of his eldest son." A man's death without a will would be a possible fact. The legal consequence of its occurrence would be the transfer of his property to the eldest son. The law would make the judgment of importance in advance of a case materializing; the only important fact would be that of a man's death without a will. The judge in such a case would not be free to decide that any other fact is important enough to justify a different legal consequence.

To elaborate, such a common law rule would take the form (or be translatable into the form) of a "when . . . , then . . . " statement. For example:

> When facts *a*, *b*, and *c* are present but fact *d* is not, then the defendant shall compensate the plaintiff for harms caused.

Such a legal rule would tell us that the presence of generic facts *a*, *b*, and *c* together with the absence of *d* shall result in the defendant's liability. The "when . . . " clause would state the factual conditions that require a court to order the legal consequence stated in the "then . . . " clause. Common law rules often are stated in a form approximating this simple scheme.

This rigid deductive form of expression can be illustrated, and its serious deficiencies in common law adjudication exposed, by an extended example.[6] Five hypothetical cases will be described as they might come up in one common law jurisdiction. The statements of fact and reasoning are simplified representations of what a court might state in a published opinion. Each story starts with Costello, the original owner of five horses and a somewhat naive and too-trusting friend of Abbott. Each horse came by theft or fraud into Abbott's hands. Costello sought a court's aid to recover possession of each horse from Abbott or someone who came into possession of the horse after Abbott sold it in turn. To help the reader keep the facts straight, a diagram of the factual relationships in each case appears as Figure 2-1.

---

[6] The illustrations are adapted from Lon L. Fuller, The Forms and Limits of Adjudication, 92 Harv. L. Rev. 353, 375-376 (1978). See also Chapter 3.

FIGURE 2-1

Case 1: Costello   →   Abbott by theft

↓

Holliday by innocent purchase

Case 2: Costello   →   Abbott by fraud

Case 3: Costello   →   Abbott by fraud

↓

Holliday by innocent purchase

Case 4: Costello   →   Abbott by fraud

↓

Holliday by purchase;
Holliday a party to the fraud

Case 5: Costello   →   Abbott by fraud

↓

Holliday by innocent purchase

↓

Ball by purchase;
Ball had heard of the fraud

CASE 1

Abbott stole Costello's horse and sold it to Holliday, who did not know and had no reason to know it had been stolen from Costello. Costello sued Holliday to recover the horse. Costello won.

The court in Case 1 might state a general rule in its opinion: A person who purchases property from a seller who did not own the property does not acquire ownership and must return the property to the rightful owner. The court then might apply the rule to the facts of the case: Holliday purchased the horse from Abbott, a thief who did not own it. Logically, this yields as a conclusion: Holliday did not acquire ownership of the horse from Abbott and must return it to Costello.

CASE 2

Abbott bought Costello's horse, giving as payment a forged check on another person's account. Abbott knew the check was forged. After delivering the horse to Abbott, Costello discovered the fraud and sued Abbott to recover the horse. Costello won.

The court in Case 2 might state another general rule: A person who acquires possession of property by fraudulent purchase does not acquire ownership and must return the property to the rightful owner. Application of the rule: Abbott acquired possession of the horse by purchase with a fraudulent check. Conclusion: Abbott did not acquire ownership of the horse and must return it to Costello. So far, so good.

CASE 3

The facts are similar to Case 2, except that Abbott sold the horse to Holliday. Holliday knew that Abbott had bought the horse from Costello, but she did not know or have any reason to know that Abbott paid with a forged check. Costello sued Holliday to recover the horse. Holliday won.

Now, if the rules stated in the precedents were "the law" that determines the results in future cases, Case 3 would have to go the other way. The combination of the rules from Cases 1 and 2 would seem to require that Costello win. Case 2 states that a person who fraudulently acquires possession of property does not acquire ownership; Case 1 states that a person without ownership of property cannot transfer ownership to another. In Case 3, Abbott did not acquire ownership of the horse, under the rule in Case 2. By finding for Holliday, the court seems to ignore the rule stated in Case 1. It finds that Holliday owns the horse when Abbott did not. (There are many cases on the books that decide Case 3 for Holliday in jurisdictions that decide Cases 1 and 2 for Costello.)

The court in Case 3 could create and state a new rule that requires the results in all three cases. It could announce, for example, that an owner of property is entitled to possession when he loses possession by another's wrongful act and seeks to recover the property from the perpetrator or from a third party purchaser when the wrongful act was theft. But surely this is quite a change from the rule given in Case 1. Moreover, this new rule would not justify the result in Case 3 based on the law stated in the precedents. Clearly, the judgment of importance—that Holliday's innocence in Case 3 is an important fact requiring a different result from the first two cases—would be made by the court in Case 3, not by the rule stated in previous cases.

How reliable, then, would be the rule stated in Case 3 for Cases 4 and 5?

CASE 4

The facts are similar to Case 3, except that Holliday had helped Abbott perpetrate the fraud on Costello. Costello sued Holliday to recover the horse.

CASE 5

The facts are similar to Case 3, except that, after buying the horse from Abbott, Holliday sold and delivered it to Ball. Ball had heard rumors of the fraud worked on Costello by Abbott. Costello sued Ball to recover the horse.

The court in Case 3 modified the rule of Case 1 to decide Case 3. The court in Case 4 similarly can modify the rule of Case 3 to decide Case 4. And the same is true in Cases 5 and so on.

Consequently, the common law process is not one of simply tracing the logical consequences of preexisting rules stated in the precedents. As Edward H. Levi put it, "[t]he rules change as the rules are applied. More important, the rules arise from a process which, while comparing fact situations, creates the rules and then applies them."[7] Judges may write as if the common law has always been what it has come to be. Some legal thinkers, such as Blackstone, thought of the common law like this. Others, such as the great Oliver Wendell Holmes, Jr., belittled views of law as a "brooding omnipresence in the sky."[8] Most of us today would reject Blackstone's view.[9]

It is misleading in another way to regard the judgment of importance as a logical function of common law rules. Reasoning by analogy would be analytically superfluous if there were previously stated rules that dictated the judgment of importance. Such a rule could simply be applied to the facts of a new case. There would be no need to search out the precedents or analyze

---

[7] Edward H. Levi, An Introduction to Legal Reasoning 3-4 (1948).

[8] Southern Pac. Co. v. Jensen, 244 U.S. 205, 218 (1917) (Holmes, J., dissenting).

[9] See, e.g., Melvin A. Eisenberg, The Nature of the Common Law (1988).

the facts of the precedents to identify similarities and differences between the precedents and the problem case. Studying cases would not be so important. Instead, we would study rules and collect them in textbooks that contained little other than the rules.

A basic principle of common law adjudication is that a judge is empowered to decide the case before the court and *only* the case before the court. A judge has no authority at common law to enact an authoritative general rule to govern parties and situations that were not before the court. Thus, the judge in Case 1 could not decide the outcome in Case 3, however broadly she may craft a rule to explain the decision in Case 1. In all likelihood, the judge in Case 1 did not consider the facts of Cases 3 et seq. when crafting the general rule. Its mechanical application in later cases may yield a thoughtless and arbitrary result. More important, the parties in the later cases are entitled to their days in court. They should not have their rights adjudicated on the basis of the facts and arguments put before the court by others in Case 1, due to the happenstance that the language employed by the court in Case 1 was sufficiently general to be so used.

These characteristics of common law adjudication are reinforced by the practice of distinguishing between the *holding* of a precedent and its *dicta*. "Holding" is commonly used in either of two senses. A broad holding is much like a common law rule, which states its factual part in general terms.[10] To minimize confusion, let us call this a "ruling." A narrow holding is more case-specific and difficult to get a handle on. For our purposes, a *holding* is a statement that captures in a sentence or two the probable significance of a single precedent as a base point for reasoning by analogy in future cases.

A holding summarizes the important case-specific facts in the precedent case and states the legal consequences then attached to those facts. The important facts are those that are likely to become a point of important similarity or difference between the precedent and a problem case. For example, the holding of Case 1 above is that an owner of property who is the victim of a theft can recover possession of the property from a third party who bought it from the thief, even if the third party did not know or have any reason

---

[10] See Chapter 4 §A.

to know that it was buying stolen property. Consider variations on the facts in Case 1. Should the result be the same if Costello is the victim of a fraud? Case 3 suggests not, so the law in Case 1 should be confined to cases involving a theft. That is all the judge had authority to decide.

Accordingly, without casting doubt on the holding in Case 1, the court in Case 3 can properly hold that an owner of property who is the victim of a fraud cannot recover possession of the property from a third party who, not knowing or having reason to know of the fraud, bought it from the perpetrator of the fraud. It thus decides that the difference between fraud and theft is an important difference that requires a different outcome. Similarly, the court in Case 4 can hold that a purchaser who helped perpe-trate a fraud on the original owner is not like the buyer in Case 3, which decided only that the owner cannot recover possession of the property from a third party who did not know and had no reason to know of the fraud. It thus decides that Case 4 is more like Case 2, in which the owner sued the perpetrator of the fraud himself, than it is like Case 3, in which the owner sued a subse-quent purchaser who was not complicit in the fraud.

A holding will be used as a base point in reasoning by analogy. It summarizes what was decided in a single case in which the judge did not and could not decide a class of cases. A holding does not determine the result in other cases involving different parties under different circumstances. Those cases will be decided when they come up. They will be treated according to the holding of a precedent if they *then* are determined to be like the precedent in the more important respects. A holding may have implications for a class of future cases. But whether a problem case is within that class will be decided when the case is brought before a court.

Common law rules stated in precedents are dicta to the extent they are broader than a case-specific statement of the important facts and the legal outcome. (Statements on points of law that need not be decided in the case are called "obiter dicta.") Dicta lack the status of legal authority because they purport to exceed the powers of a common law judge. Dicta can be useful when lawyers predict what the court will do in future cases because they often express the court's inclinations on matters expected to come before it. But the holding of a case has the privileged status of "the law." Dicta forecast, in a vague and less reliable way, what the law is likely to become.

In each case as the law unfolds, then, the general rule announced in a prior case need be given effect only to the extent that the (narrow) holding of the precedent requires. The general rule announced in Case 1 ("A person who purchases property from a seller who did not own the property does not acquire ownership and must return the property to the rightful owner") can be disregarded properly in Case 3. It is dictum to the extent it is more general than the holding ("An owner of property who is the victim of a theft can recover possession of the property from a third party who bought it from the thief, even if the third party did not know or have reason to know that it was buying stolen property"). Therefore, the best statement of a holding will change as subsequent cases are decided.

The analogical form captures significant aspects of legal reasoning at common law (and, we will see, in other settings). The Abbott and Costello sequence illustrates how the analogical form in law provides a vocabulary and frames an issue for decision, contributing to the rationality of legal thought. In Case 5, for example, a judge should decide whether one who, having heard rumors of the fraud, buys a horse from an innocent purchaser who bought it from one who took possession by fraud, is *more like* one who bought a horse fraudulently (Case 2) or from a thief (Case 1), or *more like* one who, not knowing or having reason to know of the fraud, bought a horse from one who took possession by fraud (Case 3). We would expect legal arguments in Case 5 to address that legal issue, posed in the analogical form, by parsing the analogies and disanalogies among the cases.

But what leads a court to decide, for example, that the difference between fraud and theft in Cases 1 and 3 is an important difference requiring different results? Fraud and theft are alike in some respects; both are wrongful in the eyes of the law. They are unalike in other respects: Fraud at common law is a civil wrong, not punishable by imprisonment, but theft is a criminal wrong, punishable by imprisonment. The courts often consider the difference here to be more important than the similarity, at least when the subsequent purchaser is an innocent one. Similarly, Costello is the victim of wrongful behavior in all of these cases.

The precedents are unlike Case 5 in other respects, however, because none involved a purchaser who had heard of the wrongful behavior and bought the horse from a purchaser who was wholly innocent and herself would win in a suit by the original owner. The resolution of the key issues remains a mystery, so far as the form of analogical legal reasoning suggests.[11]

Analytically, analogies leave the crucial third step—the judgment of importance—wholly unconstrained. As Professor H.L.A. Hart put it:

> [T]hough "Treat like cases alike and different cases differently" is a central element in the idea of justice, it is by itself incomplete and, until supplemented, cannot afford any determinate guide to conduct. . . . [U]ntil it is established what resemblances and differences are relevant, "Treat like cases alike" must remain an empty form. To fill it we must know when, for the purposes in hand, cases are to be regarded as alike and what differences are relevant.[12]

To be sure, in practice, some cases are so obvious that an analogy seems to suffice without supplementation. But the interesting cases will not be those.

To summarize, analogical legal reasoning—reasoning from (narrow) case holdings—is but a formal version of the analogical reasoning used in everyday life. It is governed by the principle that like cases should be decided alike and unalike cases decided unalike if the differences are important. This form of reasoning requires three steps: (1) identifying an authoritative base point, or precedent; (2) identifying factual similarities and differences between the precedent and a problem case; and (3) judging whether the factual similarities or the differences are more important and, therefore, whether to follow or distinguish the precedent. The analogical form contributes significantly to the rationality of legal thought by providing a framework for analysis, identifying starting points for reasoning, and framing a legal issue.

---

[11] For further discussion of these examples, see Chapters 4 §A and 6 §C.

[12] H.L.A. Hart, The Concept of Law 155 (1961).

However, judging which facts are more important remains a mysterious activity.

I will take up this key problem—the judgment of importance—in later chapters. Let us first consider deductive legal reasoning in an enacted law context. Deductive legal reasoning also requires a judgment of importance. We can better confront that difficult problem after you consider whether it is avoidable.

CHAPTER THREE

Deductive Legal Reasoning

LEGAL REASONING IN THE deductive form is most closely associated with reasoning from enacted law, which usually consists of general rules. Such rules are found in a variety of official legal documents, such as constitutions, statutes, codes, regulations, and executive orders.[1] These laws are enacted and published by groups of people who are authorized to make law, such as Congress, a state legislature, or executive and administrative agencies. For convenience, I will primarily discuss statutes enacted by Congress or a state legislature in this chapter. The lessons, however, largely apply to other enacted rules (and, as you will see in the next chapter, common law rules).

Deductive legal reasoning differs from analogical legal reasoning in a number of key respects. First, reasoning starts from a rule, not a case. Rules are enacted before cases governed by the rule have materialized. Second, the principle of legislative supremacy generally requires judges to play a subordinate role to the more democratic branches of government.[2] Consequently, the authoritative statement of an enacted rule remains static, as it was enacted, until the nonjudicial lawmaker amends or repeals it. Courts have no authority to reformulate enacted rules as the case law interpreting the rules unfolds. Nor may courts ignore an applicable enacted rule, which normally has superior authority to any inconsistent common law. Third, the static statement of enacted rules leads legal reasoning from such rules to focus heavily on problems of rule interpretation. The judicial task is to classify problem cases in classes of cases designated by the rules.

---

[1] This form of reasoning also is employed with rules "enacted" by private persons in the form of contracts, wills, corporate charters, and the like. What is said in this chapter applies to private law of this kind with some modifications.

[2] The principle of constitutional supremacy and the doctrine of judicial review make out an important exception to this statement. The special interpretive problems of constitutional law are generally set aside from the discussion throughout this book.

Casting legal arguments in the deductive form serves a number of valuable functions. Legal rules establish the framework of law within a legal system, setting up an elaborate classification scheme that specifies the conclusions that judges might reach. Reasoning from settled rules makes the law manageable, transforming vague questions of what is "just" into more concrete questions that are often uncontroversial. Even in contested cases, the rules at least establish the starting and ending points for argument, pose the legal issues, and establish a common language for legal discourse. Judges are duty-bound to order remedies only when and as authorized by the rules. Accordingly, plaintiffs and prosecutors bear the burden of invoking a legal rule that, if applied, will vindicate their legal claims. However, deductive legal reasoning can be highly misleading: It may seem that the rules dictate the result in a case when this is not so. Like analogical legal reasoning, deductive reasoning does not avoid the need to judge importance.

A.   The Deductive Form

Like analogical reasoning, deductive reasoning[3] is familiar in a variety of everyday nonlegal contexts. A common point of comparison is the rules of a game. In the board game "Monopoly," for example, a rule provides that any player who passes "Go" receives $200 unless that player is on his way to "Jail." It is easy to determine when a player passes "Go" and is not on his way to "Jail." That player's entitlement to $200 follows automatically. Deductive reasoning is also used extensively in more serious settings. A teacher may announce that (only and all) students who answer 90 percent or more of the questions correctly on a test will receive an "A." If Martha then answers 92 percent correctly, it should follow that she is entitled to an "A." It also follows that she is not so entitled if she answers fewer than 90 percent correctly.

Logicians call this form of reasoning a *syllogism*. Its three steps distinguish deductive from analogical reasoning. First, having taken a first look at the factual situation, you should identify a

---

[3] The term *deductive reasoning* is used here to refer to deduction in the form of a syllogism. Other kinds of deduction are far less important in legal practice.

major premise (e.g., students who score 90 percent or better on a test shall receive an "A"). Second, you should formulate a *minor premise* in the language of the major premise (Martha scored better than 90 percent). Third, you should infer the *conclusion* (Martha shall receive an "A"). The major premise is a general rule describing a class with many members, allowing a conclusion that places an individual in the class designated by the rule. By contrast, wholly analogical reasoning starts from an instance and dispenses with such general categories. A conclusion in analogical reasoning is a matter of judgment, while a deductive conclusion follows logically from the premises.

So, to use a familiar example,

MAJOR PREMISE:	All men are mortal;
MINOR PREMISE:	Socrates is a man;
CONCLUSION:	Socrates is mortal.

Crucially, a syllogism is *valid* when the conclusion must be true *if* the premises are true. Only someone who is crazy or foolish would deny that Socrates is mortal while accepting both that all men are mortal and that Socrates is a man. A syllogism is *sound*, moreover, when it is valid *and the premises in fact are true*. A valid syllogism transfers the truth of the premises to the conclusion. When a premise is false, the conclusion will be true only by coincidence.

When used properly, deductive reasoning is a powerful form of reasoning—much more powerful than the analogy. The deductive form, however, can be easily misused. It may, by its form, leave the impression that a conclusion is sound when this is far from so. Look at the following silly syllogism:

MAJOR PREMISE:	A foot has 39 inches.
MINOR PREMISE:	Susan has a foot.
CONCLUSION:	Susan has 39 inches.

The conclusion is clearly nonsense. But the language of the premises yields the language of the conclusion, mimicking a proper argument. The major premise is false. The minor premise is uncertain if, for example, Susan in fact has two feet and that matters in the context. The inference is not valid, in any event, because the meaning of *foot* is different in the major and minor premises (as, less obviously, is the meaning of *has*). Any one such error robs the conclusion of its soundness.

Legal reasoning commonly is expressed in deductive form. But a syllogism, however logical in appearance, is only as good as its premises and the logical relationship between them. Validity is necessary in legal reasoning but in itself is of trivial importance. The key problems are: (1) identifying an authoritative major premise; (2) formulating a truthful minor premise; and (3) drawing a sound conclusion.

B.   Deductive Legal Reasoning

Deductive legal reasoning, like its analogical cousin, is more formal and rigorous than similar reasoning in most everyday nonlegal contexts. For example, law practice relies on well-accepted rules that identify the authoritative major premises. Federal law is superior to state law; among federal laws, the Constitution is superior to statutes and statutes are superior to administrative rules. Among state laws, the state constitution is superior to statutes and statutes are superior to administrative rules. Due to the principle of legislative supremacy, enacted laws in principle are superior to a state's common law, which is made by judges. In general, later enactments prevail over earlier enactments when they are inconsistent.[4]

Nonetheless, serious problems can be involved in adopting the premises and establishing an appropriate relationship between them. At any point, judgments of importance akin to those required in analogical reasoning can arise. Consequently, you should learn the deductive form most carefully; if you do not, others may use it to deceive you with its pretense of iron logic.

---

[4] This neat picture of a hierarchy of laws can be misleading. There may be several plausibly applicable laws within the same plane of the hierarchy and even within the same enactment.

1.   *The Rule*

The first step in ordinary deductive reasoning is identifying a relevant major premise. Similarly, the first step in deductive legal reasoning is identifying the legal rules that govern the case at hand. Conflicts between rules aside, enacted rules themselves describe the classes of cases in which they apply. On first encounter, you may think that a rule is easy to apply. Upon careful reading and analysis, however, you will often find that this impression is misleading.

To illustrate, assume a problem case as it might appear to a lawyer from an initial interview with a client in the law office. We will work through part of the relevant statute as the lawyer might. Note that the discussion begins with the facts before searching for the applicable rule. These facts are stated wholly in ordinary, nontechnical language and give only a superficial account of what happened. After locating a plausibly applicable rule, a lawyer might have to search out additional facts in greater detail to formulate minor premises that are suitable for reasoning deductively to a conclusion. The first impression that a particular rule applies could easily be wrong.

Assume that Franny Farmer grows peaches at her small, family-run orchard in rural Georgia. She contacted Morris Auster, a buyer of produce for distribution in the Atlanta area. Farmer and Auster met on May 28 at the orchard. After inspecting the young fruits, they reached an agreement for Farmer to sell Auster 200 boxes of peaches per week for three weeks in July, from Farmer's orchard, at a price of $40.25 per box. They shook hands and departed, not having put their agreement into writing. On June 3, rural Georgia was struck by severe rain, winds, and flooding, damaging much of the state's peach crop for the season. Thinking the shortage of peaches would cause the price to rise, Auster sent a signed letter to Farmer on June 10, stating that it was "to remind you of our agreement for you to sell me 200 boxes of peaches per week for three weeks in July. $40.25 per box." Farmer did not reply. In July she sold all of her peaches to Bert Berkowitz, at $50.75 per box.

Auster sees his lawyer. He wants to sue Farmer to enforce the contract. To determine whether it would be worthwhile to litigate, Auster's lawyer needs to predict what a court is likely to do in this case. This is a commercial transaction governed by a statute known as the Uniform Commercial Code (UCC).[5] On consulting the UCC, the lawyer will find dozens of statutory sections grouped in ten general categories, called articles. Which provisions might govern Auster's case? Auster's lawyer will see that Article 2 is titled "Sales." His attention will focus here.

The lawyer will read the first provisions of Article 2 to determine whether it governs Auster's case. He will find that an early section provides that "this Article applies to transactions in goods" (§2-102). In the deductive form, he will ask if peaches are "goods" within the meaning of this provision. This is not a difficult legal issue. A nearby section of Article 2 provides that *goods* means "all things which are movable" and "includes growing crops" (§2-105(1)). The peaches in Auster's case were "growing crops" and therefore "goods" within the meaning of Article 2. It applies. Auster's lawyer has narrowed the search to the class of commercial transactions involving sales of goods and therefore to the provisions of Article 2 of the UCC. He has excluded the many rules that govern sales of land, sales of corporate stock, sales of services, other kinds of sales, and other commercial transactions.

Auster's lawyer will then read through Article 2 to further narrow the scope of his problem. On reading §2-201(1), he might be disappointed to find that a class of contracts for the sale of goods must be in writing to be enforceable:

> Except as otherwise provided in this section a contract for the sale of goods for the price of $500 or more is not enforceable . . . unless there is some writing sufficient to indicate that a contract for sale has been made between the parties and signed by the party against whom enforcement is sought.

It might appear from this rule that the Auster/Farmer contract will fall in the class of unenforceable contracts, much to Auster's chagrin. The contract is for the sale of goods at a price of more

---

[5] The Uniform Commercial Code has been enacted as statutory law in forty-nine states and the District of Columbia. It was drafted and promoted by two nongovernmental organizations of the nation's leading lawyers, judges, and legal scholars—the National Conference of Commissioners on Uniform State Laws and the American Law Institute.

than $500. Farmer is the "party against whom enforcement is sought" in the action by Auster to enforce the contract. She did not sign a writing of any kind. However, this would be a hasty conclusion: The rule applies "except as otherwise provided" in §2-201. Auster's lawyer should read on.

The second subsection of §2-201 identifies a class of contracts that are enforceable even if they are for sales of goods for $500 or more and there is no writing signed by the party against whom enforcement is sought. The rule is a fairly complicated one. It amounts to saying that some people who receive a writing confirming a deal must object to the confirmation promptly or be precluded from using §2-201(1) to defeat enforcement of the deal. Section 2-201(2) provides:

> Between merchants if within a reasonable time a writing in confirmation of the contract and sufficient against the sender is received and the party receiving it has reason to know its contents, it satisfies the requirements of subsection (1) against such party unless written notice of objection to its contents is given within ten days after it is received.

This rule might apply in Auster's case. Auster sent Farmer a letter to remind her of the deal. She did not reply. Auster's lawyer might use the rule in §2-201(2) as a major premise and formulate a minor premise that is faithful to the facts while satisfying each element of the major premise. If so, he could argue that Auster's case falls within the class of enforceable contracts designated by §2-201(2), not the class of unenforceable contracts designated by §2-201(1).

Auster's lawyer knows from these rules that to get a court to enforce the contract (so far as the requirement of a writing is concerned) he must show that the Auster/Farmer contract was "between merchants," that Auster's letter was a "writing in confirmation," that it was "received" by Farmer "within a reasonable time," and so on. Farmer's lawyer knows as well that she can block enforcement by showing that the Auster/Farmer contract was not "between merchants," or that Auster's letter was not a "writing in confirmation," or that Farmer did not "receive" the letter "within a reasonable time," and so on. A judge similarly knows that she must make a finding on each of the several issues to decide whether the requirements of §2-201(2) were met in Auster's case.

The rules as stated in an enactment, however, only identify the legal issues. Framing the issues is no small contribution. Until these issues are resolved, however, the lawyers do not know whether the Auster/Farmer contract is unenforceable by Auster because it is not in writing. The rules do not determine the scope of their own applications.

2.   The Facts

The second step in deductive legal reasoning is stating the facts in a way that allows an inference leading to a valid conclusion. Here you may confront a problem of considerable complexity: The facts in any case can be described in a variety of terms. Some plausible descriptions will fit the terms of an authoritative rule with little or no discomfort, as Farmer's peaches seem clearly to be "growing crops" and therefore "goods" within the meaning of that term in Article 2. Others, however, will fit the rule only awkwardly or with incompatible implications.

I will use Auster's case to illustrate this step as well. To focus your attention on characterizing the facts, let us simplify the issues. From the previous discussion, we can derive a somewhat unwieldy rule that can be stated as a major premise:

> MAJOR PREMISE: Whenever a contract for the sale of goods is between merchants, and within a reasonable time a writing in confirmation of the contract and sufficient against the sender was received, and the party receiving it had reason to know its contents, and notice of objection to its contents was not given within ten days after it was received, then the requirement of UCC §2-201(1) is satisfied against the recipient.

The statement of facts stipulates that Farmer did not reply to Auster's letter of June 10. Assume further that Auster's letter was a "writing in confirmation of the contract," was "sufficient against the sender," was "received" "within a reasonable time" by Farmer, and that Farmer had "reason to know its contents." A more manageable, if artificial, major premise now can be formulated for illustrative purposes:

MAJOR PREMISE: When and only when a contract is between merchants and . . . , then the requirements of §2-201(1) are satisfied against the recipient.

To reason from this premise deductively, Auster's lawyer must formulate one of two possible minor premises: Either the Auster/Farmer contract was or was not between merchants. Given the major premise, no other minor premise allows an inference to a valid conclusion. Because the two possible minor premises contradict each other, one of only two conclusions is possible: Either the requirements of §2-201(1) were or were not satisfied against Farmer. Auster will win the point only if the first minor premise is found to be true as a matter of fact.

MAJOR PREMISE: When and only when a contract is between merchants and . . . , then the requirements of §2-201(1) are satisfied against the recipient.

MINOR PREMISE₁: The Auster/Farmer contract was between merchants.	MINOR PREMISE₂: The Auster/Farmer contract was not between merchants.
CONCLUSION₁: The requirements of §2-201(1) were satisfied against Farmer.	CONCLUSION₂: The requirements of §2-201(1) were not satisfied against Farmer.

Which minor premise is true? Auster's lawyer can *say* that either is true; he can pick the one that favors his client's interest. Insofar as anyone else is concerned, however, this only identifies a logically possible minor premise. The opposite minor premise and conclusion is also logically possible. Therefore, merely *saying* that one of them is true will not convince anyone else, even if his logic is valid. In particular, Auster's lawyer will not convince a judge or Farmer's lawyer unless he establishes a sound argument based on facts that can be evidenced at a trial.

The problem, then, is to determine whether the Auster/Farmer contract in fact was "between merchants." But which of the two characterizations of the facts is proper? What facts would be relevant to a decision? The facts of a case do not come prepackaged in the language of the rule. The rule may not even contain criteria for its own application. Interpretation is surely required in any case.

3.   The Judgment of Importance

Interpretation, in the narrow sense, is the intellectual process of giving meaning to linguistic symbols, such as the words or combinations of words that are found in legal rules. Certain common problems of language make interpretation necessary. Few, if any, words have one and only one meaning so that they refer to some object in the world with certainty. Proper names come closest to that ideal. Most words, however, suffer from a lack of clarity in one or more of several ways. Words may have two or more identifiable meanings—as previously mentioned, the word *bar* is an example. Such words are called *ambiguous*. Words may have meanings that shade continuously from one to another with no line of demarcation—*orange* and *yellow* are examples. Such words are called *vague*. And groups of words in a sentence may cause similar clarity problems. In the sentence *The house had a gazebo in the yard which was yellow*, was it the house or the gazebo or the yard that was yellow? Such a lack of clarity may be called *sentence ambiguity*. All three kinds of unclear meanings can require interpretation of a legal rule.

In everyday life, we normally think of the meaning of a word as its definition. Legal definitions of legal terms can be useful in easy cases. However, interpretation through definitions often transforms the problem of interpreting a rule into a problem of interpreting the definitions of its words, transforms a problem of interpreting the definitions into one of interpreting the definitions of a definition, and so on. When the last of the available definitions is found, there may still be vagueness or ambiguity.

In Auster's case, the term *between merchants* is defined in §2-104(3) of Article 2 of the UCC:

"Between merchants" means in any transaction with respect to which both parties are chargeable with the knowledge or skill of merchants.

The case is a bit unusual because we have a statutory definition of a part of a definition. *Merchant* is defined in §2-104(1) in relevant part as follows:

"Merchant" means a person who deals in goods of the kind or otherwise holds himself out as having knowledge or skill peculiar to the practices or goods involved in the transaction. . . .

These definitions are helpful in further narrowing the scope of the problem. But they do not solve it. Auster is probably chargeable as a "merchant" because he "deals in goods of the kind." As a middleman between the growers and the Atlanta market, he probably makes several hundred produce purchases and sales and several dozen peach purchases and sales in any year. He is reasonably expected to know his trade well. Consequently, we can safely conclude, Auster should be chargeable as a "merchant."

For the contract to be enforceable against Farmer, however, "*both* parties [must] be chargeable with the knowledge and skill of merchants." It is far from clear whether Farmer is chargeable as a "merchant." She may make as few as one peach sale for a few deliveries in a year. Her orchard was described, you will recall, as a "small, family-run" business. She may not be a very sophisticated businessperson at all. Perhaps no one would expect that she should be. Farmer might "deal in goods of the kind" or might "otherwise hold [her]self out as having knowledge or skill" of the kind described. Or she might not.

The definitions are like a rule in a significant respect: The definitions themselves may require interpretation because they suffer from the problems of language. In the first part of the definition of *merchant*, the phrase *goods of the kind* may refer only to peaches or also to fruits, produce, or foodstuffs in Auster's case. This phrase is ambiguous. Moreover, Farmer might or might not deal in peaches. The word *deals* is vague because it is not known how much or what kind of business activity would make Farmer a dealer; her level of business activity is on a continuum of sorts from a consumer (who is not a merchant) to a big-time middleman like Auster (who surely is). And the phrase *between merchants* means "in any transaction with respect to which both parties are chargeable with the knowledge or skill of merchants," not more simply when both parties "are merchants." This suffers from a sort of sentence ambiguity: One who surely "deals in goods of the kind" might or might not be "chargeable with the knowledge or skill of merchants" if she does not also "hold [her]self out as having knowledge or skill peculiar to the practices or goods involved in the transaction." The definition of "between merchants" might refer to both parts of the definition of merchant, or it might refer only to the second part.

A judgment of importance is required: What facts would justify charging Farmer as a merchant because she "deals in goods of the kind"? Is Farmer more like Auster the merchant, or more like Bessie, a consumer who may make more peach purchases in a year than Farmer makes sales? Is the number of sales or purchases the important fact? The quantities involved? Is the difference between sales and purchases important? Is the fact that Auster both purchases and sells important? What about the fact that Auster and Farmer act for a profit, while Bessie does not? Is the fact that Auster deals in produce while Farmer deals—if at all—only in peaches important?

Similarly, what are the important facts that would establish whether Farmer is chargeable as a merchant because she "holds [her]self out as having knowledge or skill peculiar to the practices or goods involved in the transaction"? Must she say to Auster that she knows the business practice of sending and responding to confirming letters—the "practices . . . involved in this transaction"? Must she say to Auster that she knows produce well—the "goods involved in the transaction"? Or would it be enough that she introduced herself to him as a businesswoman who grows and sells peaches in small quantities, or that she has a sign at the entrance to her orchard announcing to the world "FRANNY'S ORCHARDS—EXPERTS IN PEACHES"?

The rules and their definitions do not point directly at the important facts in the case—those that establish whether Farmer is a merchant such that the Auster/Farmer contract was "between merchants." The rules and their definitions do not provide the particularities you need to resolve the controversy by deduction from the rule stated in §2-201(2). Moving from the rule to the definition of terms in the rule, to definitions of the definitions, keeps you in the realm of generalities. Eventually, you exhaust the rules and definitions that purport to determine which argument in a case is the correct one by deduction.[6] Then you must make a judgment of importance to classify a problem case.

To help a statutory rule perform its functions, deductive legal reasoning employs a number of source materials other than definitions. These other materials also do not supply the particularities we need. For example, some say that an unclear statute should be interpreted to give effect to the intention of the legislature. This "intention" is well known to be a fictional thing. A legislature is a group of people; groups themselves do not have intentions. The remarks in debate by a bill's floor leader or the report of a single legislative committee or a statement by a legislator at a hearing each do not necessarily represent the intention of the deliberative body as such. Lacking such necessity, deductive reasoning from such statements will not yield a necessary conclusion. Only the language of the rules is approved by the group, and that returns us to the starting point of our analysis, caught in a circle.

Moreover, if a reliable picture of the legislature's intention could be pieced together, what form would it take? It could be another general statement of what the law permits or requires in a class of cases—a rule—which circles back into the problems of language. It could be an example of the intended effect of the rule in a hypothetical or historical situation, leaving one to reason analogically and with the need to judge importance. Or it could be a statement of the rule's objective or purpose, though these, too, will be like rules or cases and circle back into the problem of importance. In any event, the "intention of the legislature" will not

---

[6] Lawyers sometimes consult a dictionary of English language which supplies, at best, another rule, which leads to the same problem one syllogism down the road. It more often supplies a number of definitions among which one must choose. The drafters of statutes often do not intend for the ordinary meaning of a word to be employed, especially when a term has been given a statutory definition that turns it into a term of art within the statute. As in the example, lawyers sometimes are less concerned with a single word than with a phrase or sentence or, as will be seen in Chapter 7, much more.

supply the particularities we need to reason deductively to a necessary conclusion in a controversial case.

A number of other kinds of guidance may be available for interpreting a statutory text. Perhaps statutes should be read as a whole to give them coherent meanings, avoiding contradictions between provisions or leaving any provision without a point. Perhaps the legislative history, including the floor debates, committee reports, and hearings before its enactment, should be taken into account. Perhaps statutes should be interpreted in light of legal history—how the common law and other legislatures treated the problem in other times and places. And perhaps statutes should be interpreted in light of the historical, economic, and social circumstances at the time of its enactment.

All of these sources of information are often helpful and in fact are used in good legal reasoning, as we will see in Chapter 4. However, the commonly expressed commandment to "take into account" such a wide variety of things generates considerable frustration. We feel that we have been told to think about everything before doing anything. That is a formula to ensure that we do nothing. We need to know *what we are looking for* in the enacted text as a whole, the complex legislative history, the centuries of legal history, or the multitude of historical, economic, and social circumstances at the time of enactment.

Surely none of these sources of information will supply the particularities we need to formulate minor premises allowing deductive reasoning from an unclear legal rule to a sound conclusion. Some may provide examples of situations (historical or hypothetical) and the "intended" effect of the general rule in those situations. Again, however, we can use that information analogically. Some may provide statements that are abstract and refer to classes of cases. That, again, will stop short of logically determining a case's membership in the abstract class. In either event, we are left with the need to judge importance.

The judgment of importance requires us to go beyond the problems of language that inhere in legal rules, definitions, and similar expressions. This should not be surprising. As indicated at the outset, a rule is an abstract or general statement of what the law permits or requires of classes of people in classes of circumstances—in classes of cases. A rule stands in contrast to a case—a short story of an incident in which the state acted or may act to settle a particular dispute. Accordingly, the language of an enacted rule, announced before any case governed by the rule has materialized, describes an abstract class. The statement of conditions (the "when . . . " clause) points at the class of cases, not at the particular facts of any problem case.

When a word like *merchant* is merely copied from the conditioning part of a major premise and placed in the position of a minor premise, it does not suddenly point at the particular facts in a case. Instead, it continues to point at a class of cases. Such a use of words leaves the minor premise, so to speak, dangling in the air. The connection between the abstract class and the case remains to be drawn; in the example, it remains to determine whether Farmer, in particular, is a member of the class of people "chargeable as merchants." And it should be drawn by some process of reasoning that is not dependent on other rules or definitions that themselves will similarly dangle. As Justice Holmes said long ago from the Supreme Court, "[g]eneral propositions do not decide concrete cases."[7]

Drawing this all-important connection—placing a case in a legal class—requires a judgment of importance to mark the particular facts that justify the classification. Deductive legal reasoning does not indicate how to make this judgment in the real-world situations that interest lawyers and judges. The form of deductive legal reasoning promises a conclusion backed by logical necessity. At least in controversial cases, the problem of characterizing the facts of a case in the language of the rule robs the syllogism of its necessity.

Like analogical legal reasoning from cases, deductive legal reasoning from rules has its uses and abuses. Good lawyers and judges neither accept these forms nor reject them as forms. They use them to benefit from their strengths and supplement them to avoid their weaknesses. You should understand their plusses and minuses if you are to make good arguments and see through bad ones. Mastering them requires you to understand, crucially, the points in reasoning where a judgment of importance remains unconstrained by officially stated legal rules or definitions.

We still must confront the judgment of importance. First,

---

[7] *Lochner v. New York*, 198 U.S. 45, 76 (1905) (Holmes, J., dissenting).

however, let us consider the relationships between the deductive and analogical forms. The combination of the two principal forms of legal reasoning contributes further to the rationality of legal thought. But it does not constrain the judgment of importance.

CHAPTER FOUR

Combining Analogies and Deductions

TO SIMPLIFY THIS introduction to law and legal reasoning, I have separated analogical and deductive reasoning too completely. True, analogical legal reasoning is characteristic of the common law, and deductive legal reasoning is characteristic of enacted law. But good lawyers also use common law rules deductively and apply enacted rules through analogical reasoning from cases and other base points. This chapter will show you how to combine the deductive and analogical forms.

Combining the two forms of legal reasoning serves some highly useful functions. When you are working through a common law problem, the analogies become increasingly unwieldy as the number of precedents increases. Common law rules allow you to express yourself economically and to organize the precedents. When you are working through an enacted law problem, you will find, the rules often lack particularities needed to determine the class to which a problem case belongs. The context, however, may include examples of the rule's intended or accepted effect. You can use these situations as base points for reasoning analogically to interpret and apply the rule.

But combining the two forms does not allow you to dodge the need to judge importance. If your resources were limited to rules, precedents, and logic, legal reasoning would send you back and forth between analogies and deductions in a regress, as when you stand between two tilted mirrors. You could start with the analogical form, reach the judgment of importance, and shift to the deductive form using a common law rule. The problem of importance, however, would reappear in the deductive form. If you start with the deductive form, reach the judgment of importance, and shift to the analogical form, the judgment of importance remains as well. This conundrum reflects how the two forms amount to two ways of expressing the same thought: Treating like cases alike, as in analogies, is much like applying rules consistently, as in deductions. Fortunately, you can escape the conundrum

by using additional resources in legal reasoning, as we shall see in
Chapters 5 and 6.

A.   Common Law Rules

In Chapter 2, we considered analogical legal reasoning in
common law cases. You learned that, in this kind of reasoning, we
(1) identify the relevant precedents, (2) compare and contrast the
facts of a problem case with the facts of the precedent cases, and
(3) judge whether the factual similarities or differences are more
important in the circumstances. The third step is the troubling one:
Judges may claim to be following a previously stated common law
rule when deciding a case. But the rule is dicta, and thus not law,
to the extent it goes beyond the previous judges' authority to
decide the case before them. Consequently, we saw, rules stated in
common law precedents do not determine the outcome in subsequent cases.

1.   Easier Cases

It would be a mistake, however, to think that common law
rules serve no useful purpose. Unlike enacted rules, common law
rules have roots in the case law: They stand for the holdings of a
group of precedents. You can refer to the group by using the
words and phrases of the common law rule. With this in mind,
you can use the rules in deductively formed arguments for
convenience in easy cases. There is no point to articulating many
obvious analogies when a simple deductive argument will satisfy
those who are concerned.

To illustrate, consider again the Abbott and Costello sequence.[1]
To refresh your memory, all of the cases concerned the rights of
the original owner of a horse (Costello) to recover possession of
the horse when possession was taken by a person (Abbott) using

---

[1] See Chapter 2 §B.

wrongful means (theft or fraud). The first three cases held that (1) an owner of property who is the victim of a theft can recover possession of the property from a third party who bought it from the thief, even if the third party did not know or have any reason to know that the property had been stolen; (2) an owner of property who is the victim of a fraud can recover possession of the property from the person who perpetrated the fraud; and (3) an owner of property who is the victim of a fraud cannot recover possession of the property from a third party who bought it from the perpetrator when the third party did not know or have any reason to know of the fraud.

The court in Case 3 might state a general rule that summarizes these three holdings: An owner of property is entitled to possession when he loses possession by another's wrongful act and seeks to recover the property from the perpetrator or from a third party purchaser when the wrongful act was theft. We know from Chapter 2 that this rule would not be reliable in some possible future cases. There are cases, however, where the rule can yield an uncontroversial conclusion—one that passes without objection among those concerned. The deductive form may be the most simple way to express the law in such cases.

For example, assume Abbott steals a horse from Costello. Costello sues Abbott to recover possession of the horse. Of course Costello should succeed, though no precedent is directly on point. Costello's lawyer may present his argument to Abbott's lawyer in the deductive form.

MAJOR PREMISE: Case 3 ruled that an owner of property is entitled to possession when he loses possession by another's wrongful act and seeks to recover possession from the perpetrator of the wrongful act or from a third party purchaser when the wrongful act was theft.

MINOR PREMISE: Costello lost possession of his horse to Abbott by theft, a wrongful act, and seeks recovery of possession from Abbott, the perpetrator.

CONCLUSION: Costello is entitled to recover possession of the horse from Abbott.

Abbott's lawyer is likely to advise Abbott to return the horse even though he knows that this conclusion is not required by the rule stated in Case 3. That rule is dicta insofar as it is broader than its roots in the precedents. Case 1 held only that the original owner can recover possession from a third party who bought it from a thief. Case 2 held only that the original owner can recover possession from the perpetrator of a fraud. Neither precedent held that the original owner can recover possession from a thief, which is the issue now presented. Abbott's lawyer, however, could not argue convincingly that this case is different from the precedents in any important respect. Rather, this case is an even clearer case requiring recovery by the original owner. Abbott's lawyer should concede the point because there is no plausible argument with which he can contest it.

The deductive reasoning in such a case is short and sweet and to the point. Full expression of the analogical reasoning yielding the same conclusion could show the obvious in a more complex and pedantic way. To do so would be unnecessary, confusing, and time consuming for all concerned.

What makes this case easy, however, is not the deductive form of Costello's argument. No court can stop the law's evolution by announcing a rule in a single case. Rather, a common law rule summarizes a number of precedents. The precedents have the superior authority: They retain their significance as base points for analogies. If a stated common law rule leads logically to a different result from the one supported analogically by its underlying precedents, then so much the worse for the common law rule.

2.   Organizing the Precedents

Common law rules have other useful functions, too. Not the least of these is providing a framework for organizing what may be dozens or hundreds of precedents. Reasoning by analogy from each and every precedent would be overwhelming. Composing an intelligible argument would be humanly impossible. To make the thought process manageable, we simplify by organizing the large number of relevant precedents into subclasses of precedents, each with fewer members. We then name each subclass with a phrase in a common law rule, which should capture the significance of the precedents it covers. You can then locate (by legal research) or refer (in argument) to that subclass of precedents quickly and easily by using the right phrase.

Consider, for example, the general common law rule governing cases in which a plaintiff seeks compensation from a defendant whose careless behavior harmed the plaintiff or the plaintiff's property. The traditional lawsuit arising at common law from an automobile accident is a familiar example. The rule, known as the common law negligence rule, may be stated as follows:

> If (1) the defendant was under a duty to use reasonable care to avoid a harm, and (2) the defendant breached that duty by a negligent act or omission, and (3) the breach of duty was a cause-in-fact and (4) a legal cause of (5) damage to the plaintiff's person or property, then the defendant shall compensate the plaintiff for such damages (unless certain exceptions not relevant here apply).[2]

In a single jurisdiction, there could be a few hundred precedents supporting this negligence rule. These precedents are organized into five subclasses, each of which is named by an element of the rule. Thus, in shorthand form, there are the (1) duty cases, (2) breach of duty cases, (3) cause-in-fact cases, (4) legal cause cases, and (5) damage cases. These subclasses are distinguished from one another by the kind of issue that was decided by the court. The precedents in each subclass should be more like each other (in respect to the issue that was decided) than they are like the precedents in the other subclasses (in the same respect).

The negligence rule indicates that, to recover compensation, the plaintiff in a negligence case must show that her situation is like that of the plaintiffs who won in all five subclasses. Assume that Georgio's car collides with Susan's when Georgio is admiring the scenery instead of watching the road. Susan's lawyer knows that, strictly speaking, five analogical arguments are necessary. She

---

[2] The distinction between *cause-in-fact* and *legal cause* (also called *proximate cause*) is not important for present purposes, as long as the reader accepts that there is a difference.

must show that (1) Susan's situation is like that of the plaintiffs who succeeded in showing that the defendant had a duty in cases where that question was decided. She must show in addition that (2) Susan's situation is like that of the plaintiffs who succeeded in showing that the defendant breached its duty in the cases where that question was decided. Susan's lawyer also must show that Susan's situation is like that of the plaintiffs who succeeded in showing that the defendant's breach of duty was (3) the cause-in-fact and (4) the legal cause of (5) the damage suffered by the plaintiff. Georgio's lawyer can defeat Susan's claim by showing that Susan's situation is unlike those of the victorious plaintiffs, or that Georgio's situation is like those of the victorious defendants, in any one of those five subclasses.

Most problem cases do not require the court to analyze the analogies in all subclasses named by a rule. The only contested issue in Susan's case might be whether the defendant's negligence was a legal cause of Susan's injury. That is, the parties might accept that Susan's situation is like that of the plaintiffs who won in the precedents encompassed by the other four elements of the rule. The court now must decide if Georgio's breach of duty was the legal cause of Susan's injury; that is, whether Susan's situation is like that of the plaintiffs who won on the legal cause issue in the legal cause cases.

Consequently, an argument at common law can be stated in the form of a legal syllogism in any case:

MAJOR PREMISE: If (1) the defendant was under a duty to use reasonable care to avoid a harm, and (2) the defendant breached that duty by a negligent act or omission, and (3) the breach of duty was a cause-in-fact and (4) a legal cause of (5) damage to the plaintiff's person or property, then the defendant shall compensate the plaintiff for such damages.

MINOR PREMISE: Georgio (1) had a duty to operate his car with reasonable care, (2) he breached this duty by failing to maintain a proper lookout, (3) which in fact caused a collision with Susan's car, (4) his breach was the legal cause of injury to Susan, and (5) it damaged Susan's foot.

CONCLUSION: Georgio shall compensate Susan for the damage to her foot.

This represents a deductive argument from the common law rule only in a limited way. The logic of the rule as stated establishes that Susan's lawyer must make five successful arguments, setting aside any question of overruling. Assuming that Susan's lawyer makes all five arguments, however, the soundness of the conclusion cannot be established by the rule and the logic alone. Because soundness depends on the underlying analogies, you must look and see whether the analogies support the minor premise. Therefore, the legal syllogism does not represent the full reasoning required to decide Susan's case. Rather, the syllogism represents abstractly the results of a highly complex web of analogical arguments from a large number of precedents.

In sum, the common law precedents are organized in a classification scheme described by the common law rules. Like enacted rules, the common law rules refer to classes of cases. Unlike enacted rules, however, common law rules refer to classes of precedents already decided by courts. Common law rules are used deductively to express conclusions economically and to identify precedents to consider analogically. Analytically, however, the action is with the underlying analogies, even when they are left unstated. Consequently, combining common law precedents and rules does not constrain the judgment of importance.

B.   Cases and Enacted Rules

You learned in Chapter 3 that legal reasoning in the deductive form requires lawyers and judges to (1) identify an authoritative and applicable rule that serves as a major premise, (2) describe the facts of a problem case in a minor premise, and (3) interpret the rule in relation to the facts to reach a sound conclusion. In many situations, however, a conclusion deduced from an enacted law is not sound. This is because, when enacted, the rules refer to classes of cases that have not yet materialized. They consequently may not supply the particularities you need to place a problem case in these classes. Classification depends on a judgment of importance that is not determined by the general language of the rule.

You can employ analogical legal reasoning to help interpret an enacted rule in relation to the facts of a problem case. Enacted rules, however, differ from common law rules because they usually lack roots in the case law. Consequently, judicial precedents using the rule are not available as base points until some time after enactment. Therefore, reasoning analogically requires other kinds of base points with which to compare and contrast a problem case. Relevant base points include both real and hypothetical situations. But not just any situation will shed light on the meaning of a rule. There should be a good reason for thinking that the situations are examples of what the rule permits or requires. Several kinds of base points can be employed meaningfully, though such base points do not have quite the authority of a precedent at common law.

The text of an enacted rule is the starting point. The text has a context that includes examples of its intended or accepted effect in concrete situations. Most obviously, the context includes the ordinary meanings of the terms used in the text. Examples that normally come to mind can be used as base points, though it is often not necessary to spell this out. Thus, if a rule prohibits anyone from bringing a "vehicle" into the city park, a normal Ford Taurus can be used as a base point for analogies to identify less obviously prohibited vehicles.

The ordinary meanings, however, tend to be helpful only in easy cases. The interesting problems are those in which the ordinary meaning of the text is vague, ambiguous, or leads to an absurd conclusion. To illustrate, consider the Speech Clause of the First Amendment to the U.S. Constitution: "Congress shall make no law . . . abridging the freedom of speech. . . . " Any lawyer reasoning from this general rule deductively can be seriously misled. For example, the language on its face expresses a prohibition only on certain acts by Congress. But, together with the Fourteenth Amendment, it also prohibits such acts by the states.[3] There is no need to digress to explain how that came about, since it is settled law for now. A more straightforward problem will be posed.

---

[3] The Speech Clause is "incorporated" into the Due Process clause of the Fourteenth Amendment, which applies by its terms to the states. See Gitlow v. New York, 268 U.S. 652 (1925); Whitney v. California, 274 U.S. 357 (1927).

Assume two problem cases.

PROTEST'S CASE:

A state enacted a statute making it a crime for anyone to hang the governor in effigy. Peter Protest was prosecuted under the penal statute for hanging the governor in effigy, which he admitted doing. Protest was convicted and sentenced to a jail term. He argued unsuccessfully in state court that his conviction was unconstitutional and should be set aside because the statute violated the Speech Clause. Protest appealed to the U.S. Supreme Court on that ground.

NIHIL'S CASE:

A state enacted a statute making it a crime with special penalties for anyone to hang the governor. Neil Nihil was prosecuted under the statute for hanging the governor, which he admitted doing. Nihil was convicted and sentenced to a jail term. He argued unsuccessfully in state court that his conviction was unconstitutional and should be set aside because the statute violated the Speech Clause. Nihil, too, appealed to the U.S. Supreme Court on that ground.

By coincidence, the two cases reach the Supreme Court at the same time. Certainly, the Supreme Court would and should set aside Protest's conviction but not Nihil's. A statute that penalizes hanging the governor in effigy abridges the freedom of speech, but a statute that penalizes hanging the governor does not. The problem is to explain the reasoning that justifies these conclusions. This may not be easy. You cannot justify setting aside Protest's conviction by an argument that also requires setting aside Nihil's. Nor can you justify convicting Nihil with an argument that also requires convicting Protest. The rule of law disallows this kind of serious inconsistency. Therefore, you must draw a distinction between the two cases.

You cannot use the text of the Speech Clause deductively to draw the needed distinction. The text leads deductively to the conclusion that both convictions should be upheld. Neither hanging the governor in effigy nor hanging the governor is speech (if "speech" is interpreted in its ordinary sense to mean talking or using words). By this approach, neither act would be protected by the First Amendment.

Fortunately, the law allows you a richer array of resources. In addition to the ordinary meanings of a text, its context includes precedent cases interpreting and applying the text, uncontroversial hypothetical cases, cases or situations governed by other rules within the same enactment, historical events or situations linked to enactment of the rule, contemporary historical, economic, and social practices at the time of enactment, and examples given in the legislative history. As we will now see, these features of context can shed light directly on the legal meaning of an enacted text.

The Supreme Court, for example, has given "freedom of speech" a broader interpretation than the ordinary meaning of "speech"—talking or using words. In *Tinker v. Des Moines School District*,[4] the Court held that a high school student who wore a black armband to a public school in 1965 to protest the Vietnam War could not be suspended from school for that reason. This protest was "symbolic speech" within the protection of the Speech Clause. In other cases, the Court has said that the First Amendment generally protects freedom of expression. Paintings, photographs, music, and other forms of expression thus may be constitutionally protected, along with lectures criticizing official policies, campaign speeches, and other more obviously protected kinds of expression.

But you cannot justify the Protest and Nihil decisions by giving "speech" the meaning *expression* (or *political expression*) and then reasoning deductively from that interpretation. You would have to conclude that both convictions should be set aside:

---

[4] 393 U.S. 503 (1969).

MAJOR PREMISE: When a state imposes a penalty for engaging in expression, then the penalty shall be set aside as a violation of the First Amendment.

MINOR PREMISE$_1$: Protest's conviction was a penalty for engaging in expression.

MINOR PREMISE$_2$: Nihil's conviction was a penalty for engaging in expression.

CONCLUSION$_1$: Protest's conviction shall be set aside.

CONCLUSION$_2$: Nihil's conviction shall be set aside.

Both hanging the governor in effigy and hanging the governor are ways of expressing political views. The latter is but a way to express them forcefully. The mere fact that expression, even political expression, is a part of Protest's purpose does not justify setting aside Protest's conviction. The same argument requires setting aside Nihil's conviction, which surely would be absurd.

You might better distinguish the two convictions by introducing some analogies. For example, you could interpret the Speech Clause in light of an analogy between the two problem cases and a precedent case that construed the same enacted rule, such as *Tinker*. Thus, Protest's conviction might be set aside because hanging the governor in effigy is like wearing a black armband to protest the Vietnam War. *Tinker* and Protest's case both involve expressions of dissenting political views by symbolic means that should be allowed in a democracy. The differences between wearing a black armband and hanging a governor in effigy do not seem important. Nihil's act of hanging the governor, by contrast, was violent, physically harmful, and antidemocratic. It is different from *Tinker* and Protest's case in a way that justifies a difference in outcome.

Additionally, you might reason by analogy from uncontroversial hypothetical cases suggested by your imagination. Hanging the governor in effigy is like giving a public lecture criticizing the governor's policies. Such a lecture is surely protected by the First

Amendment. By contrast, hanging the governor is more like hanging one's spouse, usually a clear case of murder. Hanging one's spouse, too, is expression in some respects: Ask a psychoanalyst. Yet the First Amendment does not protect murder.

A third kind of base point for analogies—cases or situations governed by other rules within the same enactment—might also support the needed distinction. The Speech Clause is joined in the First Amendment with the Press Clause: "Congress shall make no law . . . abridging the freedom of speech, or the press. . . . " Neither Protest nor Nihil was exercising freedom of the press, so that clause does not apply. It probably would apply, however, to protect a published political cartoon depicting the governor hanging from a tree, in effigy or in the flesh. Hanging the governor in effigy is in important respects like such a published political cartoon. Hanging the governor is not. You could thus look to cases or situations governed by other rules within the context of the Speech Clause. Perhaps the entire Constitution should be interpreted to give it a coherent meaning, either because the drafters should be presumed to have intended a coherent document or because a coherent constitution is a better constitution.

You might find other useful base points in historical events or situations linked to the enactment of a rule like the Speech Clause. The history of events that inspired the First Amendment is part of its context. A colonial government's suppression of Peter Zenger's expressions of political criticism, for example, is the sort of thing the First Amendment was designed to prevent. The suppression of Zenger's press was recalled during the debates preceding ratification and often compared to unwanted English practices in the colonies.[5] You might justify the two decisions by reasoning that hanging the governor in effigy is like what Zenger did but hanging the governor is not. Some such reasoning might underlie *Tinker*. Wearing a black armband to protest the Vietnam War is much like what Zenger did.

Analogies to situations in the context can support decisions at surprisingly sharp odds with the ordinary meaning of a legal text. Perhaps no case illustrates this possibility better than the one that

---

[5] Zaccariah Chaffee, Free Speech in the United States 21 (1969).

follows, which also illustrates additional base points from the context. In 1885, Congress enacted a statute making it

> unlawful for any person . . . or corporation . . . in any manner whatsoever, to prepay the transportation, or in any way assist or encourage the importation or migration of any alien or aliens, any foreigner or foreigners, into the United States . . . under contract . . . to perform labor or service of any kind in the United States. . . . [6]

The Church of the Holy Trinity, a corporation in New York, made a contract in 1887 with E. Walpole Warren, then an alien living in England. The contract required Warren to move to New York and enter into service as the rector and pastor of the church. The church was prosecuted for violating the statute, which prescribed a fine as the penalty for its violation.

The lower court reasoned that the church had prepaid the transportation for Warren to come to the United States to perform the services of rector and pastor. Therefore, it concluded, the statute had been violated.[7] The deductive validity of the lower court's reasoning was impeccable.

Nonetheless, the U.S. Supreme Court reversed.[8] Writing for the Court, Justice Brewer conceded that "the act of the corporation [was] within the letter of this section, for the relation of a rector to his church is one of service. . . . "[9] However, he made two analogical arguments to justify the Court's conclusion that performing pastoral services in New York was not performing "labor or service of any kind in the United States," within the meaning of the statute.

First, Justice Brewer considered "contemporaneous events, the situation as it existed, and as it was pressed upon the attention of the legislative body,"[10] to identify the perceived problem that the statute was intended to rectify. He found that

---

[6] 23 Stat. 332 ch. 164 (1885).
[7] United States v. Church of the Holy Trinity, 36 F. 303, 303-304 (1888).
[8] Church of the Holy Trinity v. United States, 143 U.S. 457 (1892).
[9] Id. at 458.
[10] Id. at 463.

[t]he motives and history of the act are matters of common knowledge. It had become the practice for large capitalists in this country to contract with their agents abroad for the shipment of great numbers of an ignorant and servile class of foreign laborers, under contracts, by which the employer agreed, on the one hand, to prepay their passage, while, upon the other hand, the laborers agreed to work after their arrival for a certain time at a low rate of wages.[11]

Second, Justice Brewer considered the statute's legislative history. He found that the responsible Senate committee recommended enactment to the full Senate, but in its report expressed a preference for amending the language to substitute the words "manual labor" or "manual services" for the expressions "labor" or "service" wherever they appeared. The committee did not so recommend, the report said, because the committee expected the courts to interpret the statute to include only manual laborers, and the committee wanted a quick adoption of the statute in the final days before congressional adjournment. So it would appear that the Senate sought to prohibit importation of manual laborers, but not others. The responsible House committee had made similar remarks.

The Court concluded that the church's contract with Warren was not legally like the contracts to import manual labor. Justice Brewer quoted from the House committee's report in describing the important features of the base point situation:

[T]hey come here under contract to labor for a certain number of years; they are ignorant of our social condition, and that they may remain so they are isolated and prevented from coming in contact with Americans. They are generally from the lowest social stratum, and live upon the coarsest food and in hovels of a character before unknown to American workmen. They, as a rule, do not become citizens, and are certainly not a desirable acquisition to the body politic. The inevitable tendency of their presence among us is to degrade American labor, and to reduce it to the level of the imported pauper labor.[12]

---

[11] Id. at 463 (quoting United States v. Craig, 28 F. 795, 798 (1886)).
[12] Id.

He pointed out a distinction for ministers: "It was never suggested that we had in this country a surplus of brain toilers, and least of all, that the market for the services of Christian ministers was depressed by foreign competition."[13] Consequently, his opinion concluded: "So far, then, as the evil which was sought to be remedied interprets the statute, it also guides to an exclusion of this contract from the penalties of the act."[14]

In other words, Justice Brewer identified from contemporary historical, economic, and social practices and from the legislative history a relevant base point for reasoning by analogy. "Cheap immigrant labor" is the kind of situation prohibited by the statute. He identified the similarity between that situation and the problem case: Both involved contracts to bring aliens to the United States to perform labor or services here. He also identified the differences between the two situations: Warren's arrival would not "degrade American labor." The Court concluded that the differences were more important than the similarity. Accordingly, the lower court's decision was reversed, despite its airtight logic.

In sum, analysis of enacted law begins in any case with an authoritative rule as stated—the text. The rule, however, does not necessarily govern deductively according to its ordinary meaning. Cases may be decided by reasoning analogically to interpret and apply the enacted rule. Because enacted rules lack roots in the case law, however, such analogical reasoning requires base point situations found in the context of the enactment. There are at least seven features of the context that may contain useful base points: (1) the ordinary meanings of the words of an enactment, (2) judicial precedents applying the same enacted rule,[15] (3) noncontroversial hypothetical cases, (4) cases or situations governed by other rules in the same enactment, (5) historical events or situations linked to the enactment, (6) contemporary economic and social practices at the time of enactment, and (7) the legislative history.

---

[13] Id. at 464.

[14] Id. If the language of the statute and parts of the Supreme Court opinion strike you as poor English, be assured that I agree.

[15] Note, however, that the force of precedent need not be the same in common law, statutory, and constitutional cases. See Edward H. Levi, The Sovereignty of the Courts, 50 U. Chi. L. Rev. 679 (1983).

Of course, these resources may yield conflicting analogies, and they may not be helpful in some cases. Even when they help, however, you do not avoid the judgment of importance. Each analogy presents or re-presents that crucial judgment. Combining the forms of legal reasoning simply moves the judgment to another place in the reasoning. Even in combination, rules and precedents do not determine legal results based on facts and logic alone.

C.   Detour on the Judicial Role

From the foregoing discussion, you may wonder whether the courts have too much power to expand or restrict the apparent meaning of a duly enacted law. In the examples, the Court expanded the Speech Clause to protect expression or political expression when the First Amendment said "speech." The Court restricted the immigration statute to prohibit importing only manual labor and services when it said "labor or services of any kind." But the principle of legislative supremacy generally requires judges to play a subordinate role to the more democratic branches of government. Similarly, principles of constitutional democracy require the judges to interpret and apply the Constitution, not to make new constitutional law. How can these cases be right?

The need to interpret general enactments can allow judges to exceed their lawful authority even when starting with authoritative rules. Judges are reasoning much like a conscientious legislator when they consider all possible analogies and decide on the basis of how all of them should be treated. Overuse of analogical reasoning, therefore, can elevate the judiciary to a more powerful position than most of us consider acceptable in our system of government. This brings the legitimacy of the judicial practice into question.

Legitimacy will be considered in Chapter 9. Here, we observe that the constitutional doctrine of a separation of powers often leaves it unclear whether a question should be resolved by the judicial or legislative branch. In practice, it seems, the courts decline to act on all possible analogies when doing so tends to establish what the law should be, not what it is.[16] Courts may decline for this reason to apply an enacted law as called for by an intellectually appealing analogical argument, applying instead the enacted law using the ordinary meaning of the text.

In *McBoyle v. United States*,[17] for example, the defendant was convicted of violating a 1919 federal statute prohibiting any person from knowingly transporting a stolen motor vehicle across state lines.[18] McBoyle transported from Illinois to Oklahoma an airplane he knew to have been stolen. The statute defined the term *motor vehicle* as follows:

> The term "motor vehicle" shall include an automobile, automobile truck, automobile wagon, motorcycle, or any other self-propelled vehicle not designed for running on rails.[19]

An airplane is not commonly called a "motor vehicle." It probably would not fall within the above definition, according to the ordinary meaning of the words in 1919.

You could argue that an airplane should be treated as a "motor vehicle" for purposes of this statute. An airplane can be analogized to an automobile or truck and is a "self-propelled vehicle not designed for running on rails." Here is the analogy: Automobiles and trucks were included in this federal enactment because they can so easily be taken outside the state in which they were stolen. When this happens, state law enforcement officials are hampered because their jurisdiction ends at the border. This is not a problem for the feds, whose jurisdiction covers the nation. Like automobiles and trucks, a stolen airplane can easily be taken outside the state in which it was stolen. Consequently, it may be argued, airplanes should be classified as "motor vehicles" because they are legally like automobiles and trucks for purposes of this statute.

Justice Holmes, writing for the U.S. Supreme Court, acknowledged the force of this analogy. He refused, however, to uphold McBoyle's conviction:

---

[16] This Introduction is not the place to consider the highly complex practices of judicial restraint in constitutional cases.

[17] 283 U.S. 25 (1931).

[18] 41 Stat. 324 (1919).

[19] Id. at §2(a).

[T]he statute should not be extended to aircraft, simply because it may seem to us that a similar policy applies, or upon the speculation that, if the legislature had thought of it, very likely broader words would have been used.[20]

Holmes reasoned that "vehicle," in everyday speech, calls up the picture of a thing moving on land. He insisted that, when criminal penalties are involved, a fair warning should be given to the world, in language common people understand, of what the law intends to do. For this reason, Holmes refused to follow the analogy and expand the statute's coverage beyond its apparent meaning.

Holmes's approach to the statute in *McBoyle* stands in contrast to Justice Brewer's in *Church of the Holy Trinity*. You may be tempted to think that either Holmes or Brewer has the better position in general. This would be a mistake. The restrained judicial role exemplified by *McBoyle* may be appropriate to several kinds of statutory cases. Our tradition suggests that criminal statutes like the one in *McBoyle* should not be expanded by the use of analogies.[21] As Holmes pointed out, the rules of the criminal law should give reasonable notice to the public of what will constitute an infraction. Keeping to the ordinary meaning of the words furthers that goal. Some spending statutes are another example. The power of Congress to control the federal budget is basic to the U.S. system of government. The judiciary rightly hesitates to intrude on Congress's prerogative to authorize expenditures of taxpayers' dollars. Moreover, many judges occasionally follow a rule of interpretation requiring a court to follow the plain meaning of a statute that is clear and unambiguous on its face.[22]

The more expansive judicial role exemplified by *Church of the*

---

[20] 283 U.S. 25, 27 (1931).

[21] Note that Justice Brewer did not expand the criminal statute's scope in *Church of the Holy Trinity*.

[22] See, generally, Karl N. Llewelyn, Remarks on the Theory of Appellate Decision and the Rules or Canons About How Statutes are to be Construed, 3 Vand. L. Rev. 495 (1950); Arthur M. Murphy, Old Maxims Never Die: The "Plain Meaning Rule" and Statutory Interpretation in the "Modern" Federal Courts, 75 Colum. L. Rev. 1299 (1975).

Holy Trinity also is appropriate to several kinds of statutory cases. For example, commercial questions, such as those raised by Auster's case in Chapter 3, do not enjoy much political priority on the legislative agenda. For this reason, legislatures often want the courts to continue developing areas like commercial law, as they have traditionally. Cases involving statutes protecting minority rights, such as the civil rights laws, may require a more active judicial role. It is one thing to say to the U.S. Department of Justice, as Justice Holmes effectively did in *McBoyle*, that it should make its argument to Congress. It is quite another to say the same thing to a lone victim of racial or other similar discrimination.

My purpose is not to delineate a theory about when the courts should apply statutory rules according to the ordinary meanings of the words, leaving a wider range of arguments to the more political branches of government. Enough has been said to suggest that both approaches play—and should play—significant roles in statutory cases. A judge's approach is often informed, to a large extent, by her conception of the proper judicial role in relation to the legislature's. That role is not the same in all statutory cases. In fact, judges often subordinate their role to that of the legislature, as Holmes did in *McBoyle*.

To summarize the main points of this chapter, the deductive and analogical forms of legal reasoning may be combined in cases governed by both common law and enacted law. Common law rules may be used in the deductive form to express the conclusion in easy cases economically. They also are used in the deductive form to identify the legal issues by organizing the relevant precedents. However, legal reasoning in the analogical form remains the underlying mode of thought. Similarly, analogical reasoning may be used to help interpret and apply an enacted rule. The analysis begins with the enacted text. It may help to find base points in the context that can be used to reason analogically in a problem case.

Even together, however, the two forms do not solve the key problem that neither solves alone. Switching at every difficult point to the other form of reasoning does not solve the problem of judging importance. Rules and cases, used deductively or by analogy, do not seem able to constrain that judgment. Holmes was eloquent in describing the need for additional legal resources:

[T]he logical method and form flatter that longing for certainty and for repose which is in every human mind. But certainty generally is illusion, and repose is not the destiny of man. Behind the logical form lies a judgment as to the relative worth and importance of competing legislative grounds, often an inarticulate and unconscious judgment, it is true, and yet the very root and nerve of the whole proceeding. You can give any conclusion a logical form. . . . But why do you [do] it?[23]

He was less helpful in explaining how the judgment of importance can be constrained by the law so that judicial decisions are made within the rule of law. Let us now confront that crucial problem.

---

[23] Oliver Wendell Holmes, Jr., The Path of the Law, 10 Harv. L. Rev. 457, 466 (1897).

CHAPTER FIVE

Legal Reasons and Conventions

THE UNAVOIDABLE judgment of importance requires a judge to determine which of the many facts in a case should count in judicial deliberations as reasons for placing a case in the classes designated by legal rules. A *legal reason* consists of a fact together with a legal standard that makes that fact important as a guide to action for law-abiding people. Thus a red light, together with the legal rule requiring motorists to stop at red lights, is a legal reason for a motorist to stop. It is also a reason for a judge to classify a motorist who ran a red light as a violator of the traffic code, and a reason to fine the motorist as provided therein. Judges should consider the legal reasons, pro and con, bearing on each decision they make. They should decide based on the stronger reasons in the circumstances.

The rules and precedents considered in preceding chapters are among the legal standards that can generate legal reasons. We have seen that these resources for reasoning may not suffice—separately or in combination—to constrain a judgment of importance within the law. In the next three chapters, you will find that additional resources are available for legal reasoning. In this chapter, I will introduce the professional conventions that support legal principles and policies, which will then be presented in the next two chapters. Together, these chapters show you how judicial decisions may draw on all of these legal resources to decide cases coherently according to the law. Your legal arguments should draw on these additional legal resources as well as on rules and precedents.

A. Is Legal Reasoning Scientific?

We begin this phase by dipping briefly into the philosophy of law and legal reasoning. In my experience, many beginning law students (and others) have difficulty grasping law and legal reasoning because they expect something that law and legal reasoning cannot and should not deliver. Specifically, they expect the law and legal reasoning to function like a modern scientific enterprise. The remarkable successes of the physical and mathematical sciences understandably inspire people in other fields to follow or adapt the methods of reasoning they think are employed in the most successful fields. Often, however, it is a romanticized version of scientific reasoning that dominates thinking about what is rational.[1] Without digressing to discuss more accurate views of science, let me suggest that the laws of a society should not be used as a scientist might use the laws of nature. When we distinguish scientific and legal reasoning carefully, we make additional resources available to help you solve legal problems.

A scientific kind of reasoning may seem implicit in the deductive and analogical forms of legal reasoning. The popular conception of scientific reasoning focuses on a potential relationship of correspondence between a word or symbol in a scientific proposition and an objectively ascertainable (observable) fact in the empirical world. The proposition is supposed to state the conditions under which natural events occur. For example, one may hypothesize that water changes from liquid to gas when heated to 212° F, using a thermometer to gauge the temperature. Following a number of such observations, one might formulate the proposition that water always boils when heated to 212° F. If on some occasion water does not boil at 212° F, one might conclude that the thermometer is broken or that another relevant condition, such as atmospheric pressure, has changed. In the latter case, the proposition might be reformulated to say that water always boils at 212° F when the atmospheric pressure is the same as at sea level. Predictions then could be made with greater confidence by looking for two observable facts corresponding to the two conditions in the proposition. In a sound scientific proposition, on this conception, the two conditions should be necessary and (jointly) sufficient conditions for water to boil. All cases of boiling water would have

---

[1] "It is a commonplace of the philosophy of science that evidence is incomplete, that alternative hypotheses and possibilities can be imagined, that theories are held tentatively until a better one is produced, and so on." Robert Nozick, Philosophical Explanations 23 (1981). See also Thomas Kuhn, The Structure of Scientific Revolutions (2d ed. 1970).

two empirical facts—temperature and atmospheric pressure—in common.

The two forms of legal reasoning might seem to involve a similar kind of reasoning. Deductive legal reasoning uses a rule as a major premise that appears to state the necessary and sufficient factual conditions for any case to fall within the class designated by the rule. The common law negligence rule, for example, requires a defendant to compensate a plaintiff if the defendant (1) was under a duty to use reasonable care, (2) breached that duty, which breach was the (3) cause-in-fact and (4) legal cause of (5) damage to the plaintiff. This seems to suggest by its form that compensation is required in any case in which five empirical facts are present and not when one or more are absent—that all cases of negligence have these facts in common. (Note, however, that the five conditions state legal conclusions, not facts in any empirical sense!)

The analogical form also seems to presuppose a kind of reasoning like the popular conception of scientific reasoning. You might think that two cases are alike and should be treated alike under stare decisis if they have material facts in common.[2] Assume that a precedent case includes facts *a, b,* and *c* but *not-d,* and the court holds that the plaintiff must compensate the defendant. A problem case also includes facts *a, b,* and *c* but *not-d.* You might say that the plaintiff should compensate the defendant because the two cases have facts *a, b,* and *c* but *not-d* in common; therefore, they are like cases that should be treated alike. However, you could as easily say as a rule that the plaintiff must compensate the defendant whenever facts *a, b,* and *c* but *not-d* are present. The rule is implicit in the analogy.

Despite these formal similarities, you should resist any temptation to believe that legal reasoning should mimic this conception of scientific reasoning. Below, I will offer two arguments for this. First, scientific and legal reasoning have such different functions that the formal similarities are overwhelmed by

---

[2] See, e.g., Harry W. Jones, John M. Kernochan, & Arthur W. Murphy, Legal Method 6 (1980); E. Levi, An Introduction to Legal Reasoning 3 (1948); Jack L. Landau, Logic for Lawyers, 13 Pacific L.J. 59, 77-78 (1981); Herman Oliphant, A Return to Stare Decisis, 14 A.B.A.J. 71, 72 (1928).

the differences. Second, law cases that are members of the same legal class need not have all—or even any—facts in common.

B.   The Normative Function of Law

Respected legal scholars have conceived of legal reasoning along the lines of the popular conception of scientific reasoning described above. Most prominently, Christopher Columbus Langdell, originator of the socratic method of law instruction in the late nineteenth century, sought to place the law on a scientific and conceptual footing. The lore is that, for Langdell, the law consisted of objective, neutral, and determinate rules that dictate single correct results in all possible cases.[3] Holmes rebelled against Langdell's conceptualism, proclaiming that "the life of the law has not been logic, it has been experience."[4] He treated the law as predictions of judicial behavior and aspired to place it on an empirical scientific basis. In the early twentieth century, "legal realists" reconceived law as a social science that should capture the observable regularities in official behavior.[5] More recently, members of the critical legal studies movement have argued, among other things, that because legal reasoning fails to obey causal laws, the law is pervasively indeterminate.[6]

This intellectual history is recounted because of its legacy—skepticism about law and legal reasoning among many legal academics. For different reasons, beginning law students tend to find themselves similarly skeptical early in the first year of law school: Good students learn quickly that little law involves the straightforward application of legal rules. Though that lesson is valuable, you might jump from there to skepticism because you think that law must either operate scientifically or else count for

---

[3] See Thomas C. Grey, Langdell's Orthodoxy, 45 U. Pitt. L. Rev. 1 (1983).

[4] Oliver Wendell Holmes, Jr., The Common Law 5 (Mark DeWolfe Howe ed. 1963).

[5] E.g., Karl N. Llewellyn, Some Realism About Realism, 44 Harv. L. Rev. 1222 (1931); Walter W. Cook, Scientific Method and the Law, 13 A.B.A.J. 303, 309 (1927). This approach to law, a part of "legal realism," stems from Oliver Wendell Holmes, Jr., The Path of the Law, 10 Harv. L. Rev. 457 (1897).

[6] E.g., Robert W. Gordon, Critical Legal Histories, 36 Stan. L. Rev. 57 (1984).

nothing. In my view, however, that jump would be unwarranted.

My first argument for rejecting the popular scientific model is that scientific and legal reasoning serve different functions requiring differences in how they are used. Propositions of the empirical sciences function to describe, explain, and predict events and relationships in the empirical world. Hypotheses are offered and tested by observation to confirm or refute their accuracy qua descriptions, explanations, and predictions, as suggested by the boiling water example in the preceding section. Accordingly, empirical sciences use a language of data, measurement, probability, verification, statistical significance, and the like, reflecting their interest in empirical events and causal relationships.

The empirical sciences stand in contrast to the mathematical sciences, which do not function to describe, explain, and predict events and relationships in the empirical world. Instead, ordinary mathematics works out the analytical relationships among numbers. It proceeds in terms of units, equality, proof, transitivity, infinity, recursion, and the like, reflecting the entities and relationships of interest to mathematicians. Mathematics in principle requires warrants for all inferences in a rigorous proof.

It would, of course, be silly to criticize a mathematical claim for lacking empirical support. Empirical investigations can neither confirm nor refute mathematical truths, which make no empirical claims. Such a criticism would be beside the point due to the difference in function. Similarly, it may be that legal (and ethical) reasoning is not vulnerable to the criticism that legal rules fail to dictate right results or describe causal laws. As math is not the kind of thing to be criticized for lacking empirical support, law may not be the kind of thing to be criticized for lacking comprehensive determinacy of results. If this were so, skepticism about law and legal reasoning would not flow so easily from the logical and causal indeterminacies in the law.

Propositions of law differ fundamentally from propositions of the empirical sciences: They do not describe, explain, or predict anything. Instead, laws guide conduct by *prescribing* lawful behavior; that is, they are *normative*.[7] For example, the law says

---

[7] Normativity here has nothing to do with the social scientist's norm, which refers to the average or typical behavior in a group. In some communities, the use of cocaine may be common enough to be "the norm" in a social scientific

that motorists should stop on encountering a red traffic light and go on a green one. Imagine yourself in the driver's seat when you encounter a traffic signal—not on the curbside observing the correlation between changing traffic lights and traffic in the aggregate. Now, you have a choice. The colored light, together with the relevant legal rule, is a *reason* for you to stop or go as indicated. It is not a description, explanation, or prediction of your behavior. It is normative because it guides your conduct.

To be sure, lawyers sometimes need to predict how judges will decide cases. Their predictions, however, should take into account that, from the judge's point of view, the law prescribes judicial conduct. Judges are not involved in predicting what they themselves shall do. They have the capacity to deliberate on what they ought to do and to act rationally and intentionally as a practical matter. The outcomes of lawsuits are supposed to be reached by legal reasoning—identifying and considering the legal reasons for and against each proposed action. A judge's judgments and orders are not determined by scientific laws, such as those that determine the paths of comets.

Accordingly, to perform their function, law and legal reasoning use a language of rights, duties, principles, responsibilities, excuses, and the like. Reference is made basically to reasons for action, not reasons for belief, as in the sciences. Legal reasoning mainly involves argument about what someone should do, not proof or experimentation, as in the sciences. It focuses on the best of the available alternative actions in concrete circumstances, not verifiable generalities, as in the sciences. A scientist can conclude that the answer to a question remains unknown for decades or centuries; however, a judge should decide a law case according to the law and without undue delay. Because legal reasoning is used to solve problems when decisions must be made, scientific criteria for its success are as inapposite as empirical findings are for a mathematician.

It need not bother you that the law does not identify legal results as laws of nature identify outcomes of experiments. The difference leaves us free to formulate laws to help make our world

---

sense. Surely that does not make it lawful. Normativity also is distinct from feelings or beliefs about appropriate conduct. See Chapter 9, note 8.

a better place in which to live. Distinguishing legal and scientific laws, however, only opens the door for a practical approach to law and legal reasoning. It does not show how the judgment of importance can be constrained by the law. First, however, let us consider a second argument for abandoning the popular scientific model of legal reasoning.

C.   Family-Style Relations Among Cases

My second and more important argument for rejecting the popular scientific model is that law cases can be members of the same legal class even when they do not have all material facts in common. It would make sense to adapt that scientific model to the legal function only if two criteria are satisfied: (1) all law cases that should be decided alike must have empirical facts in common; and (2) the common facts must correspond to the words of legal rules so that, by their presence, they signal how cases should be classified. Alas, the facts of law cases do not organize themselves so neatly.

To illustrate, consider two easy cases. Each case is governed by a common law rule requiring all contracts to be performed in good faith. The court in each was asked to decide whether a contract party breached by failing to perform in good faith. Though the cases were decided by different courts at different times, the pair of cases should be alike in the important respects to justify decisions that both parties breached by performing in bad faith.

In the first case,[8] the Vanadium Corporation contracted to purchase from Horace Reddington certain mining rights to land belonging to the Navaho Tribe on its reservation in Arizona. Because federal law required the Secretary of the Interior's approval before such rights could be transferred, the contract parties agreed that Vanadium could call off the deal if the Secretary did not approve it within six months. Vanadium promptly entered negotiations with two other people to purchase

---

[8] Vanadium Corp. of America v. Fidelity & Deposit Corp., 159 F.2d 105 (2d Cir. 1947).

other mining rights to the same lands, without which use of Reddington's mining rights would be hampered. These negotiations fell through, and Vanadium's interest in the Reddington mining rights cooled. Vanadium refused to give requested assurances to the Secretary that it would cooperate with the owners of the other mining rights, withdrew its request for approval of the contract, and asked the Secretary to disapprove its application formally. The Secretary did so. Vanadium claimed that it therefore had the right to call off the deal.

In the second case,[9] a Mr. Fry entered a contract to purchase a residential home in California. As is usual in such contracts, the deal was concluded before Fry had obtained a mortgage loan. He was given a right to call off the deal if he could not obtain a loan on terms described in the contract. Fry was advised by the real estate agent that he could not get a loan on the required terms from a bank, but probably could get one from a mortgage company. Fry delayed for some time before he applied for a loan, and he then applied only to two banks, both of which denied his applications. He told the real estate agent that he had lost all interest in the home because he had decided to move to Hawaii. Fry claimed he had the right to call off the deal because he could not obtain a loan as required by the contract.

The courts found that neither Vanadium nor Fry had a right to call off the deal. Each court said that the buyer was required by the law to perform its contract in good faith—Vanadium to attempt in good faith to obtain the Secretary of the Interior's approval, Fry to put forward a good faith effort to obtain a mortgage loan on the terms specified. Each court found that the buyer had failed to perform its contract in good faith and therefore was in breach.

Lawyers and judges would generally agree that Vanadium and Fry were both in breach for failing to perform in good faith. The problem is to explain why this is so. Significantly, there is no single nontrivial empirical fact that the *Vanadium* and *Fry* cases have in common and that signals their proper classification as contract breaches. If it were regarded as a fact that each buyer had a change of mind after concluding the deal, and for that reason

---

[9] Fry v. George Elkins Realty Co., 162 Cal. App. 2d 256 (1958).

tried to call the deal off, the search for an observable fact in common would not end. Descriptions of mental states depend on inferences drawn from observable facts, such as what the subject says or does; the statement that each buyer had a change of mind cannot be justified by pointing to observable facts that the two cases have in common. Hence, the judicial decisions cannot be justified by pointing to a common mental state (if that were conceivable) as the common fact that signals a breach of contract. Good faith, like most legal concepts, is not an observable fact, nor can it be reduced (without remainder) to necessary and sufficient conditions that are observable facts.[10]

As indicated in Section A above, the popular scientific model requires cases to be classified together when they have the important facts in common. It breaks down when *Vanadium* and *Fry* are juxtaposed. But what does make sense of their common classification?

I suggest that cases falling within a legal class are alike the way members of a family are alike, insofar as we may know.[11] No two members of most families will be alike in *all* respects, nor must any two members of most families be alike in any distinctive respect. In the nuclear family, the parents usually do not share any observable physical features in common such that the presence of those features signals their membership in the same family. Two siblings from those parents, however, will probably share some features with each parent and some features with each other. They are recognizable as members of one family, though all four do not have any distinguishing characteristic in common. A family-style relation can be modelled as follows: *A* shares characteristics with *B*; *B* shares characteristics with *C*; *A* does not share any nontrivial characteristic with *C*. *A* and *C* may belong in the same classification.

Now reconsider the *Vanadium* and *Fry* cases in light of a hypothetical third case. Ms. Vanafry concluded a contract to purchase a retail store from which she planned to sell groceries. As is common in such contracts, Vanafry was given a right to call off

---

[10] See generally Steven J. Burton & Eric G. Andersen, Contractual Good Faith (1995).

[11] See Ludwig Wittgenstein, Philosophical Investigations §§65-76 (G. Anscombe trans. 1958).

the deal if she could not obtain a mortgage loan on terms specified in the contract. Vanafry duly applied for a loan. She then entered negotiations with the owner of the neighboring property in order to purchase it. This was necessary to her plan because she needed a parking lot. Vanafry called off negotiations when the owners of the neighboring property refused to sell but offered a long-term lease. Vanafry had won the state lottery in the meantime. She then refused to give the lender requested assurances that she would acquire adequate parking space, withdrew her application for a loan, and requested the lender to make a formal determination that the loan request was denied. The lender did so. Vanafry claims that she has a right to call off the deal because she could not obtain a loan as required by the contract.

You will quickly see that the hypothetical case has some facts in common with the *Vanadium* case, others in common with the *Fry* case, and yet others that are not shared with either. It seems clear that Vanafry, too, performed her contract in bad faith. The *Vanafry* case can link the *Vanadium* and *Fry* cases, strengthening our intuition that *Vanadium* and *Fry* are akin. It is like a child in a family that links the parents as members of the family. Thus, the three cases may be members of the same legal class, even if there are no common facts that signal their proper legal classification.

The example, of course, is simplified for purposes of illustration. For each legal class of cases, all possible members may be related as are the members of a large extended family viewed over many generations past, present, and future. There are an unknown number of possible members, and the members that are known are not necessarily typical of the entire membership. Additionally, each case can be linked to several legal classes, as each person is a member of several extended families. Some cases are even like stepchildren, adopted children, and children born out of wedlock. Moreover, though legal classes are like families in the foregoing respects, they are also unlike many families in important respects. There is nothing that links cases as genes link most members of most families: Membership is assigned by human beings (judges). Nonetheless, you may find it helpful to think of the members of legal classes as the members of a family. It is more realistic, and it steers you away from the popular model of scientific reasoning.

D.   Formalism, Skepticism, and Conventionalism

The idea of family-style relations among cases captures what you need to grasp if you are to understand legal reasoning well. The family metaphor should help you see why legal rules and precedents often do not dictate the correct result in a case: The cases are too richly different for legal rules to dictate results without leading to absurdities. At the same time, the members of a class are too related for their grouping to be arbitrary. Therefore, you need to understand how a grouping can be nonarbitrary when it is not dictated by rules and precedents. Put another way, family-style relations are composed of webs of analogies linking the members of a legal class. The problem of importance, now seen in a more complex and elaborate way, arises pervasively within the web.

This way of framing the problem is not universally shared by law teachers. In general, there are two alternatives, which I will pose starkly. First, you could insist dogmatically that legal rules must dictate the results in all cases decided within the rule of law. This would endorse classical legal formalism. It would require sharply restricting the domain of law-governed activity from what it has been throughout the last several centuries. In particular, taken seriously, it would require judicial abstinence in almost all of the great cases generally thought to have contributed centrally to greater social justice in the United States.[12] It would also restrict much of the statutory and common law. For this reason, even those who uphold legal formalism in the abstract seldom follow through on its full implications in all cases.[13]

Second, you could take family-style relations to indicate that legal rules and precedents count for little or nothing. Rather, as skeptics have recently urged most significantly, law should be considered a form of politics. Judges, then, would decide cases according to their own views of social justice, manipulating the rules and other legal authorities as necessary to create the illusion

---

[12] E.g., Brown v. Board of Education, 347 U.S. 483 (1954).
[13] See, e.g., Antonin Scalia, The Rule of Law as a Law of Rules, 56 U. Chi. L. Rev. 1175 (1989).

of a rule of law.[14] This skeptical approach expands the judicial power far beyond its historic scope, setting up judges as philosopher kings to rule without effective legal constraints. It gives up on the rule of law in the hope that judges will see social justice acceptably on a regular basis. Probably most of us doubt that this is a safe bet.

A third approach, elaborated in subsequent chapters and elsewhere,[15] does not suppose that the law must dictate results or count for nothing, as do legal formalism and legal skepticism. Instead, I will build on the idea that the law constrains the judgment of importance by allowing and disallowing *reasons* to count in judicial and other legal deliberations. Reasons allowed by the law may compete. Judges must weigh them under the circumstances in each case to reach a lawful conclusion in that case. But other kinds of reasons—such as those stemming from a judge's personal interests, prejudices, and religious or moral views—would be ruled out.

Once we refocus attention from results to reasons, a richer and more practical understanding of law and legal reasoning comes into view. The law may be seen to constrain official decisions by restricting the allowable reasons for official action, even when it does not dictate outcomes. Legal reasoning may be seen as the process of using legal reasons in legal arguments, even when the arguments leave a judge to make a judgment. Legal standards can latch onto facts to yield legal reasons without necessarily requiring results. The law thus may include precedents and legal rules of the kind introduced earlier, though with tempered force. As suggested in the next chapter, the law may also include principles and policies embedded in the law, which do not pretend to dictate outcomes. And the legal standards—precedents, rules, principles, and policies—may come together in a decision constrained as to its lawfulness by the background conventions of the practice. This third approach may be called "conventionalism" because it shifts from the abstract form of law and legal reasoning to the functions they perform as they are used by members of the legal community.

---

[14] See, e.g., Duncan Kennedy, Freedom and Constraint in Adjudication: A Critical Phenomenology, 36 J. Leg. Educ., 518-562 (1987).

[15] E.g., Steven J. Burton, Judging in Good Faith (1992).

Despite important differences, lawyers and judges share much in common. As Roscoe Pound observed,

> It is an everyday experience of those who study judicial decisions that the results are usually sound, whether the reasoning from which the results purport to flow is sound or not. The trained intuition of the judge continually leads him to right results for which he is puzzled to give unimpeachable legal reasons.[16]

Similar observations are commonplace. While a judge on the New York Court of Appeals, the highest court in New York, Benjamin Cardozo reported:

> Of the cases that come before the court in which I sit, a majority, I think, could not, with semblance of reason, be decided in any way but one. The law and its application alike are plain. Such cases are predestined, so to speak, to affirmance without opinion.[17]

More recently, Judge Jon O. Newman of the U.S. Court of Appeals for the Second Circuit reported that dissenting votes were cast in only 3.7 percent of all cases decided by federal courts of appeal in the year ending June 30, 1983.[18] Even a highly critical observer like Professor Duncan Kennedy reports that "It's endlessly the case that the judge's approach to the problem strikes me as intelligent and that . . . the judge comes up with a rule which, when I think about it, strikes me as a good idea for the very reasons that he gave for it."[19]

This suggests that judges and those who study judicial decisions share understandings that often lead them to the same result, even when that result is not a necessary product of the rules and precedents. This is most plausible when we consider all cases

---

[16] Roscoe Pound, The Theory of Judicial Decision, 36 Harv. L. Rev. 940, 951 (1923).

[17] Benjamin Cardozo, The Nature of the Judicial Process 164 (1921).

[18] Jon O. Newman, Between Legal Realism and Neutral Principles: The Legitimacy of Institutional Values, 72 Calif. L. Rev. 200, 204 (1984). Of course, a few judges may not dissent every time they disagree.

[19] Duncan Kennedy, Address at the AALS Annual Meeting, Section on Jurisprudence (Jan. 7, 1986).

that arise or could arise, instead of focusing only on the few cases decided by appellate courts, much less the fewer in law school casebooks. The controversial cases discussed in the popular press and law school classrooms do not fairly represent the extent of agreement on settled points of law. In fact, the law is applied every time a lawyer advises a client and, for that matter, every time a motorist stops at a red light. Few people face difficult questions when deciding, for example, whether they are legally required to file an income tax return. In *Vanadium* and *Fry*, lawyers and judges generally would agree that the buyers breached their contracts by performing in bad faith. They might give differing explanations or no articulate explanation at all. But the results are conventionally accepted within the professional community.

You could understand this extensive agreement in practice by focusing on the relative homogeneity of the legal profession in contrast with the general populace. Perhaps the profession shares a self-interested ideology that accounts for widespread agreement within it.[20] Surely the profession remains less than fully reflective of the general populace in terms of race and gender. However, it is too diverse in terms of politics, religion, economic views, and moral philosophies for homogeneity to be a good explanation.

Lawyers and judges commonly distinguish their personal views of what the law should be from their professional views of what the law now in force permits or requires. There may be no controversy in our time so intractable as the one concerning abortion rights. Nonetheless, friends and foes of abortion rights agree that the prevailing law guarantees women a right to choose abortion in many circumstances. One side finds in this a strong motivation to seek legal change. The other resists. Both agree that the issue is one of legal change because they agree on what the law now is, despite their moral conflict. Similarly, within the legal community, you will find far more agreement on what the prevailing law permits or requires than on its justice. Accordingly, the law can be interpreted and applied as a professional matter even while its wisdom is in dispute.

---

[20] See, e.g., Joseph W. Singer, The Player and the Cards: Nihilism and Legal Theory, 94 Yale L.J. 1 (1984).

Let us call the points of general agreement among members of the legal community *legal conventions*. The parties to these conventions are judges and lawyers most centrally and, in appropriate cases, legislators, executive or administrative officials, and sometimes others. The conventions consist of the *practices and dispositions* of the parties. The practices are the collection of solutions that have been reached for legal problems in the past. The dispositions are the members' propensities to agree on the legal outcomes in possible cases in the future.[21] Dispositions are revealed only after lawyers have immersed themselves in the facts and law of cases and thought their way through to deliberate conclusions. For this reason, decided cases, published scholarly articles, treatises, and similar works better indicate professional dispositions than opinion polls of lawyers. Because they include dispositions, conventions can guide decisions even when the cases were not the subject of any explicit agreement before they arose for decision.

Conventions support interpretations of the legal materials, allowing lawyers and judges to select conventionally accepted meanings and implications from among all logically possible meanings and implications. The existence of legal conventions is evidenced by the many clear and uncontroversial cases, especially those in which results are not dictated by rules and precedents. Legal conventions are necessary for a legal system to exist under the rule of law. By most accounts, the rule of law requires more regularity in official conduct than rules and precedents can establish alone.

Conventional practices and dispositions characterize the legal community adequately to treat it as a distinctive interpretive community whose job is to interpret the law (among its functions). As you will see, professional conventions support the use of legal precedents, rules, principles, and policies to decide problem cases, thereby coordinating decisions in the aggregate to implement the rule of law. The law in a case is developed from the legal materials

---

[21] For a different conventionalist view, see Owen M. Fiss, Objectivity and Interpretation, 34 Stan. L. Rev. 739 (1982); Owen M. Fiss, Conventionalism, 58 S. Cal. L. Rev. 177 (1985) (conventions as disciplining rules). See also Jules L. Coleman & Brian Leiter, Determinacy, Objectivity and Authority, 142 U. Pa. L. Rev. 549, 622-632 (1993).

consulted in the course of legal research—case reports, constitutions, statutes, administrative regulations, treatises, law review articles, and the like. These materials represent the practices and evidence the dispositions of the legal community.

An important caveat to avoid misunderstanding: On this view, a legal decision may be right in relation to the conventions of the legal community. But it does not follow that the decision is right in any stronger sense. The decision also can be evaluated in relation to various moral, religious, economic, and political conventions or abstract theories of justice and political morality. An act may be *lawful* whether or not the law is just.[22]

Legal reasoning aims to identify lawful actions according to the law in force in a society, leaving it to critical reasoning whether that law is deserving of respect by obedience. Separate but equal educational facilities were constitutional in the United States until 1954.[23] Legal reasoning could then be used to determine what the law permitted and required, as it can be used today for the same purpose with a different result. Legal reasoning has practical value to those who want to know when they or another run afoul of the law in force.

From a critical standpoint, moreover, legal reasoning can be used to identify important objects for criticism. The law in force, as it is applied, is surely a more important target than any professor's pet theory. It may be highly deserving of debunking. In my view, for example, racial segregation was all the more odious when it was required by the law and enforced by legal means. That experience is a clear object lesson for us: The law is not always just, and it can be used as an instrument of oppression. Legal reasoning is not adequate to either defend or debunk prevailing legal practices.

The interpretive conventions support a practice that calls attention to the facts in a problem case that are likely to be regarded as important facts by other members of the legal community. The conventions can help you make reasonably reliable predictions and effective legal arguments, as they help judges make responsible decisions that may earn respect as law, at

---

[22] For elaboration, see Chapter 9 §B.

[23] Brown v. Board of Education, 347 U.S. 483 (1954); Plessy v. Ferguson, 163 U.S. 537 (1896).

least within the profession. We can allow that the currently prevailing legal conventions may support practices that are unjust and deserving of change—even radical change. Nonetheless, the prevailing conventions of the legal community may be useful because they can help you get somewhere you want to go.

CHAPTER SIX

Purposes

LET ME NOW ILLUSTRATE how judgments of importance depend on what the relevant law is trying to do. Rules and precedents are not only efforts to settle disputes. We could do that by flipping coins, at considerably less expense. Rules and precedents set standards of lawful conduct that are supposed to help make our world a better place in which to live. To do this, rules and precedents implement the law's vision of a better society. Put differently, laws have *purposes*: They implement, and should be justified by, desirable *principles* and *policies*.[1] The distinctions among rules, principles, and policies are controversial among legal philosophers. I will not get into the technical debates here. However, let me suggest the following as a working hypothesis.[2]

In a legal system, the framework of law is described by legal rules which, as you now know, designate classes of cases and affix concrete legal consequences to membership in the classes. Like legal rules, principles and policies say something about how people should act, though in a more general way. Principles and policies, however, do not set up legal classes and fix legal consequences. Rather, they provide justifications for the rules and also legal reasons for placing cases in legal classes set up by the rules. A judgment of importance may be constrained by the law when it furthers the purposes that a rule is supposed to serve (that is, implements the principles and policies that justify the rule). Consequently, you can use principles and policies from within the law to interpret and apply legal rules, treating problem cases as occasions for implementing the law's vision of a better society.

---

[1] For convenience, I will often refer to "purposes" instead of "principles and policies."

[2] For contrasting views of rules, principles, and policies, see Ronald Dworkin, Taking Rights Seriously (1978); Ronald Dworkin, Law's Empire (1986); Frederick Schauer, Playing by the Rules (1992).

A.   The Judgment of Importance

Without attending to a law's purposes, judicial decisions might be based on any facts that happen to loom largest to a judge at the time. Often, importance would flow from the judge's political preferences and interests, identification with a party, or from the happenstance of the language from a legal rule that was announced in some other context. Decisions on these bases are arbitrary in relation to any conception of justice. The law's purposes, by contrast, can be used to coordinate the activities of judges so their decisions together might have the regularity required by the rule of law. Principles and policies can call some facts to the foreground of the totality of the circumstances, leaving others in the background as context.

The judgment of importance is the decision on which of the many facts in a case justify placing that case in a legal class. Absent a theory about what the rules and precedents are trying to do, the congeries of facts in a case are puzzling. There are so many! Each fact by itself is just that—a fact. *Any* fact might be important or unimportant. It merits special attention only if it counts more than others, and it counts more than others only if it is valued for more than its truth. A fact can be so valued if it plausibly fits with a normative theory about what the law is trying to do.

To start with a nonlegal example, imagine that you are asked to tell a true story about the Mississippi River.[3] If you are told nothing more, you might be puzzled. You can tell stories about the Mississippi's length, the volume of water it carries, its contributions to irrigation, the drainage basin it serves, the facilities and sites along its banks, its propensity to flood, its role in political boundaries, its effects on human settlement patterns, the traffic it carries, the pollution it carries, its geological history, its role in *Huckleberry Finn*, the hazards of navigating it, and so on. An almost infinite number of facts about the Mississippi could be gathered. You may not know where to begin, where to end, or how to organize your story intelligently.

Now imagine that you are asked to tell a story about the

---

[3] This example is suggested by James B. White, The Legal Imagination: Studies in the Nature of Legal Thought and Expression 3-34 (1973).

Mississippi River because you want to transport grain from St. Louis to New Orleans by barge. Given this purpose, you will at once turn attention to the river's length, the navigational hazards one might encounter, and the facilities along its banks for servicing barge transports. These and related facts will merit special notice in light of your purpose. Other facts fall away from attention. They are not important for this purpose.

By contrast, imagine that you are asked to tell a story about the Mississippi because you want to locate oil deposits. You will turn attention now to its geological history. Given this purpose, you should focus on the transport of sediments into the Gulf of Mexico eons ago. Geological theories indicate that there consequently might be oil there. Now *these* and related facts about the Mississippi will come to the foreground of the totality of the circumstances. These facts are important for this purpose.

A lawyer is similarly puzzled when he first approaches a law case. So many facts can be gathered and described in so many ways! Without a theory about the relevant law's purposes, it is hard to know where to begin, where to stop, or how to organize a statement of the facts that will communicate all and only what is needed to do the job.

Suppose that you are a lawyer who is visited by a prospective client, Marilyn Mother. Mother tells you that she is divorced, works in the home, and had one child until last week. Tommy Trucker then was driving a truck down Main Street. As he approached Chestnut Avenue near her home, her son pursued a ball into the street. A collision occurred and the boy was killed. Mother wants to sue Trucker and wants you to represent her. Before deciding to do so, you will want to get some idea of what is involved by gathering the relevant facts. You should begin by questioning Mother.

What questions will you ask? At first you might be puzzled. How old was the boy? What was his name? Why was he given that name? Why did he enter the street? Was it nighttime or daytime? Did he look both ways? What was he wearing? Was he a good student? Did Mother see the collision? Is she capable of bearing more children? What kind of truck was Trucker driving? What color was it? How fast was he going? Did he wear glasses? What is his religion? Was he watching where he was going? Did he brake? Were his brakes in good working order? Did he carry insurance? Was an ambulance promptly called to the scene? Did the ambulance reach the hospital quickly? Was medical care properly administered? Absent a purpose, any of the facts found in answer to these questions, and many others, might be important. The fact that the child was a boy, not a girl, looms as large or as small as any other fact.

Consider the probable effect of two of the several possible purposes that may justify the rules in the relevant area of the common law. One theory (a deterrence theory) supposes that the law in cases like this should discourage people from behaving unreasonably when they might cause harm to others. To implement this purpose, the law forces people to compensate those who are avoidably injured by unreasonably dangerous behavior. This purpose calls your attention to Trucker's behavior. In its light, it is probably important that Trucker was not wearing his glasses, was not watching where he was going, did not keep his brakes in good repair, failed to slow down when he saw the boy's ball roll into the street, and the like. If the law's purpose is to discourage unreasonably dangerous behavior, these behaviors should be discouraged by forcing Trucker and others to pay compensation to their victims on such a basis. The fact that Trucker was driving a truck, however, is probably not important. The law does not try to discourage people from driving trucks.

By contrast, a second possible theory (a loss spreading theory) supposes that the law should spread the losses resulting from accidents among large numbers of people instead of leaving the victim to cover the losses alone. This theory might suggest that people who are more likely to have insurance should compensate victims who are less likely to have insurance. In its light, it is probably important that Trucker was driving a truck and the victim was a child. Truck drivers generally carry insurance for accidents. Children do not, and many parents do not carry insurance to cover their children when they are pedestrians. Trucker's insurance company can pay compensation to Mother and spread the cost among a large group of subscribers. For this purpose, it is not important whether Trucker was wearing glasses, was watching where he was going, kept his brakes in good repair, slowed down when a child's ball rolled into the street, and the like.

Assume it were to turn out that Trucker was driving a truck

and the victim was a child, and also that Trucker was wearing his glasses, was watching where he was going, had just inspected his brakes, braked as soon as any good driver would, and in all other respects was proceeding safely down the street. If the courts employ the deterrence theory, you should conclude that Trucker probably will not be held liable. The facts indicating that he was behaving safely are important because he did nothing that was unreasonably dangerous and should be discouraged. If the courts employ the loss spreading theory, however, you should conclude that Trucker probably will be held liable. The fact that he was driving a truck that hit a child is important because Trucker would seem to be in the best position to spread the loss among a large group of people through insurance.

Thus, the principles and policies that justify the relevant rules establish a perspective that calls the important facts into prominence. The law's purposes therefore should play a crucial role when you decide what questions to ask Marilyn Mother. They should play a similar role when you try to predict what a court would do or to persuade others of what a court should do in the case.

In addition to purposes, the legal rules themselves are supposed to call the important facts into prominence. Some elements of some rules do a reasonable job of capturing in language the significance of the class of cases for which they stand. These rules perform this function well in easier cases. Assume that Trucker had behaved in a less than perfectly safe manner in that he had failed to have his brakes inspected when they were due for an inspection a week before the accident. Assume further that the common law negligence rule governs this case: Trucker is liable if he was under a duty to use reasonable care and breached that duty, which breach was a cause-in-fact and legal cause of damage to Mother.

The language of this rule makes it fairly clear that you should focus attention on the potential causal relationship between the accident and Trucker's failure to have his brakes inspected. Because Trucker behaved safely in all respects except in failing to have his brakes inspected, that is the only possible breach of duty. The rule tells the lawyer that the breach of duty must be the "cause-in-fact" of the accident if Trucker is to be held liable under this rule. In other words, he will not be held liable if the accident would have occurred even if the brakes had been inspected. Accordingly, important facts include whether a defect in the brakes would have been discovered on inspection and whether, if discovered and repaired, the truck would have come to a stop sooner, before hitting the child. In an easy case, there may be no need to resort to the law's purposes to apply at least some elements of the rule.

Often, however, the elements of legal rules do not do a good job of capturing the important aspects of the cases they govern. As stated, for example, the language of the negligence rule does not call attention to the facts that matter when you decide whether Trucker's failure to have his brakes inspected was a "breach of duty to use reasonable care." The language of this element of the rule suggests that less than perfectly safe behavior is not a breach of duty if it nonetheless was reasonable behavior. But it does not indicate how much less than perfect is unreasonable.

If you interpret the language in light of the deterrence theory, you might focus on the fact that people commonly treat the due date for a brake inspection somewhat casually. A week's delay is not generally regarded as unreasonably unsafe behavior that the law should discourage; what people generally do in such circumstances is probably important for this purpose. However, if you interpret the language in light of the loss spreading theory, as courts sometimes do, you would reach a different result. The theory may lead a judge to seize on the imperfect behavior at least to allow a jury to find Trucker liable. What people generally do in such circumstances is not so important. That the loss probably falls on Mother alone, but could be spread by Trucker, is important. Again, the law's purpose should be a crucial ingredient in your legal reasoning: The principles and policies that justify a law provide a normative perspective that calls the important facts into prominence.

B.   General Purposes of Law

To avoid misunderstanding, I should comment further on the law's purposes. In the aggregate, legal rules, principles and policies should describe a possible world to be brought into existence by the coordinated actions of citizens and the state. The traffic laws, for example, represent a complex set of coordinated actions that should be taken by motorists in response to various colored lights and signs with various shapes. It is not hard to imagine that world. To a remarkably large extent, motorists are guided by the law to take those actions and thus to realize the traffic laws' vision in the real world. Of course, other laws, like those prohibiting the sale or use of illicit drugs, are notoriously ineffective. The social world is brought into conformity with such laws, if at all, when legal sanctions (enforced losses of liberty or property imposed for disobedience) are imposed on violators.

We assume that society would be different if the law did not exist. People generally abide by the law due to a habit of compliance and a sense of obligation, or to the practical threat of its sanctions, or from both kinds of motive. People in many situations would not behave in the same ways if there were no formal expressions of what the society regards as minimally honorable behavior and no organized criticism, such as sanctions, for misbehavior. We also assume that society generally is better off because the law exists. The laws should encourage valued behavior, discourage disvalued behavior, and guide conduct accordingly. If the laws have an effect on society, they should help make it a better society in which to live.

The abstractness of this broad perspective can be reduced somewhat by identifying two frequently competing general purposes underlying the largest part of the law.[4] First, the law should contribute to a more orderly society. People at times will find themselves in conflict in any society with any form of social organization. Serious conflicts sometimes would result in fights, feuds, and the useless destruction of life and property; if left unsettled, even nonviolent disputes can be highly disruptive to the disputants and others. Society would be better off if serious conflicts more often were resolved peacefully. An offer of peaceful dispute settlement procedures, such as adjudication, may induce many people to seek peaceful resolutions of serious conflicts that are not settled by other means.

---

[4] These, in turn, will help generate more concrete purposes tied to specific laws, which purposes are of far greater practical value in particular cases. See §C, below.

A society could settle persistent disputes in a number of peaceful and less costly ways not involving cases, rules, lawyers, and courts. Many societies in many times and places have used such alternatives, and some are being used increasingly in the United States for some kinds of disputes. For example, we could flip coins, appoint a "wise" man to rule by fiat, leave disputants to work out their differences by negotiation, or leave them to agree to employ third parties to mediate or arbitrate privately, insofar as they can without a compulsory backup. The law, however, is trying to do more than settle disputes peacefully. There is a reason why, when the disputants persist, much more costly public and compulsory dispute settlement procedures are available.

The reason is that the law should also contribute to a more just society. Absent the law, the distribution of valued liberties, properties, and dignities presumably would be a function of the relative power of each person. Society is better off if the strong at least sometimes are restrained from dominating the weak. We hope that some of our laws are effective in helping to give all people a fair opportunity to pursue their chosen ends, consistent with the liberties, properties, and dignities of others.

One or the other of these values may be emphasized in different legal systems or in a single legal system at different times. A legal system that pursued order without justice would tend toward a police state—Mussolini's Italy is an example. A legal system that pursued justice without order would tend toward chaos, as did China's Cultural Revolution. At present, the U.S. legal system is committed to both values in some sort of balance.

Though these general purposes of the law are obvious and abstract, they have practical implications for law and legal reasoning. Most members of the legal community hold as an ideal that each legal rule and each law case should further the purposes of the law as a social institution. Rules and cases thus should contribute to the maintenance and growth of a more orderly and just society. We know that we often fall short of these ideals. We nonetheless strive for them, one case at a time.

Judges are striving to promote these broad ideals of the law as well. When trying to predict judicial decisions, you should gauge how your client's activities will appear to the judge in light of these ideals, as they are implemented by the relevant rules and precedents. When persuading judges and others, you can show

how a judgment for your client helps to promote these ideals while a judgment for the opponent tends to hinder them. A judge can safely assume that members of the legal community, and the broader society, value a legal system that contributes to a more orderly and just society. Judicial decisions that so contribute are more likely to earn respect as law.

You may wonder whether the ideals of the law are too broad and too vague to help in a particular case. How do we *know* which decision will enhance social order or contribute to a more just society? Must we not first believe that an ideal Orderly and Just Society somehow "exists"? Must we first answer the questions that philosophers have failed to answer in the millennia since Plato asked them? Do we not, in fact, disagree too widely on the most basic terms of a good social life?

Let us distinguish two sorts of questions. The question "What is the ideal Orderly and Just Society?" involves many difficult and controversial philosophical questions that are of little immediate value to practicing lawyers and judges. As I see it, a major point of law is to relieve us from the daunting task of resolving our disputes by solving those problems. Contrast the practical question, "What will members of the legal community generally take to be required by an orderly and just society in this case and like cases?" This is a question about the considered judgments of people in a legal culture concerning a practical problem. The practical question may be of great value to practicing lawyers and judges: It directs us toward tentative answers in the conventions of a highly practical profession, not in philosophy.

C.   Purposes Embedded in the Legal Experience

Given a case, you can develop useful theories about the law's purposes in a number of ways. The most useful purposes are embedded in the legal experience—the existing common law precedents and rules and the enacted texts with their contexts. You will find other useful purposes in the concurring and dissenting opinions of judges or the secondary literature, including treatises, restatements of the law, and law reviews. These sources, too, for the most part draw their inferences from the legal experience, though some advocate legal change and others are academic.

Embedded purposes are reliable indications of the legal conventions. Like judges, you need not judge importance on the basis of your own value preferences or philosophical views. Instead, you can judge importance in a way that furthers the law's purposes, implementing its principles and policies, for better or worse.

1.   Purposes in the Common Law

To illustrate the play of purpose in common law cases, recall that the principle of stare decisis requires judges to follow precedent analogically. Having identified the relevant precedents and the factual similarities and differences between the precedents and a problem case, the analogical form leaves judges to decide whether the similarities or differences are more important under the circumstances. You now have seen that principles and policies help make the judgment of importance by calling attention to the important factual relationships between cases.

Recall also the line of horse trading cases in Chapter 2. I will use two of them as if they were precedents for the purpose of discussing a third as if it were a problem case. For your convenience, the facts are repeated.[5]

CASE 2
(Precedent)

Abbott bought Costello's horse, giving as payment a forged check on another person's account. Abbott knew the check was forged. After delivering the horse to Abbott, Costello discovered the fraud and sued Abbott to recover the horse. Costello won.

---

[5] You may find it helpful to refer back to Figure 2-1, page 33.

CASE 3
(Precedent)

The facts are similar to Case 2, except that Abbott sold the horse to Holliday. Holliday knew that Abbott had bought the horse from Costello, but she did not know or have any reason to know that Abbott paid with a forged check. Costello sued Holliday to recover the horse. Holliday won.

CASE 5
(Problem)

The facts are similar to Case 3, except that, after buying the horse from Abbott, Holliday sold and delivered it to Ball. Ball had heard rumors of the fraud worked on Costello by Abbott. Costello sued Ball to recover the horse.

Analogically, the legal issue in Case 5 is whether it is more like Case 2, where Costello recovered possession of the horse from Abbott, or more like Case 3, where Costello did not recover possession from Holliday. Case 5 may be more like Case 3 if the fact that Ball bought from an innocent purchaser is more important than the fact that Ball had heard rumors of the fraud. It may be more like Case 2, however, if the fact that Ball had heard rumors of the fraud is more important than the fact that Ball bought from an innocent purchaser. The decision in Case 5 turns on whether it is more important that Ball had heard rumors of the fraud or that Ball had bought from an innocent purchaser.

It is not obvious whether Costello should be more careful about being defrauded or Ball should look into the rumors of fraud and refrain from buying tainted property. The judge in Case 5, however, is unlikely to judge importance in Case 5 apart from the legal experience. Judicial decisions would not be coordinated if the judges were to make their decisions without legal basis. The law would not implement any social vision at all, and people would find it difficult to plan their transactions to avoid running afoul of the law. In case of disputes, fewer settlements would occur while the court docket would grow, delaying the delivery of justice to all. Each case should not be decided ad hoc, in isolation.

Moreover, the law would not be just if judges were to decide each case ad hoc. Basic to any concept of justice is formal justice, the principle of equal treatment under the law, which requires that like cases be treated alike and that rules be applied consistently. Dispensing with this principle leaves judges free to indulge their personal values, prejudices, ideologies, and whims without pause. Consequently, some judges might use the power of the state to oppress the odd, the unpopular or the weak; others might use official power to rob from the rich and give to the poor. One might question whether such a society settled its disputes according to law at all.

The judge in Case 5 is more likely to ask, if only implicitly, what members of the legal community generally would take to be required by an orderly and just society in Case 5 and like cases. Cases 2 and 3, of course, are like Case 5 in some respects. What the judges decided in those cases (together with the rest of the legal experience) is a fairly reliable indication of the legal community's considered judgments. The judges in those cases held that the defrauded owner can recover possession of the horse from the perpetrator of the fraud (Abbott), but not from an innocent purchaser from the perpetrator (Holliday). The judge's objective is to decide Case 5 in a way that permits Cases 2, 3, and 5 to be reconciled so that the law does not require Ball to act differently from how *anyone* should act, given the same circumstances. Accordingly, all three cases would be decided consistently under principles and policies that together may contribute to a more orderly and just society. Because Cases 2 and 3 were decided by earlier courts, the judge in Case 5 should work presumptively with purposes furthered by those decisions, if any. The judge in Case 5 should make the judgment of importance in a way that makes sense for the entire family of cases.

The principles and policies implemented by Cases 2 and 3 may not be hard to discern. Preliminarily, it should be noted that the holding in Case 2 "rights the wrong" perpetrated by Abbott on Costello by requiring Abbott to return the horse to Costello. But this will not do as a principle for Case 5. A principle that the law should "right all wrongs" hardly survives Case 3. Costello was as wronged in Case 3 as in Case 2, but Costello did not recover the horse.

The better theory in Case 2—one that is also compatible with Case 3—is that the law here tries to enhance the security of an owner of property as against others with no claim of right. One function of a system of property rights is to encourage owners to invest in maintaining and improving their property, increasing the aggregate wealth of society. Some people would be less likely to spend time, money, and other resources on maintaining and improving property if another person could take the property without the voluntary consent of the investor. In Case 2, forcing Abbott to return the horse allows Costello to reap the benefits of ownership as expected. Abbott has no claim of right because there is no apparent reason why the perpetrator of a fraud should retain possession of the horse.

This understanding of Case 2 is consistent with Case 3 because there are countervailing reasons why Holliday should retain possession of the horse. The law also seeks to encourage people to buy and sell property, thereby increasing the aggregate wealth of society through trade. Purchasers like Holliday would be less likely to buy property if they could lose possession to a prior owner who had been defrauded by another, perhaps long ago. In Case 3 Holliday paid a price for the horse and relied reasonably on receiving ownership and possession. She did not know and had no reason to know that Abbott obtained possession of the horse by fraud. Allowing Holliday to keep possession of the horse furthers the goal of encouraging trade; allowing Costello to recover possession might discourage some people like Holliday from trading. Consequently, Holliday should receive the benefit of her bargain.

A judge in Case 3 need not deny that holding for Holliday might tend to discourage owners like Costello from maintaining and improving their property. In this case, however, there is no way to avoid hurting one of them unfairly. (Abbott cannot be sued because, typically, he has flown the coop.) As between Holliday and Costello, Costello might have protected himself while Holliday could not. People like Costello should be encouraged to be more careful about detecting fraud in the transactions to which they are parties. Therefore, Holliday stands in greater need of the law's protection.

To complete the story, in light of this understanding of the law's purposes, Costello has a plausible argument for recovering possession in Case 5. Ball had heard rumors of the fraud. Unlike Holliday in Case 3, it was possible for her to protect herself. Consequently, Costello's appeal to the security of ownership is stronger against Ball than it was against Holliday in Case 3.

Ball, however, has a stronger argument than Costello in Case 5. The law in these circumstances seeks to increase the wealth of society by enhancing the security of owners and innocent purchasers of property. When these two goals conflict, as in Case 3, the law gives preference to the security of innocent purchasers when the original owner is defrauded by another. The preference for protecting the security of innocent purchasers is likely to carry over to Case 5, to Ball's advantage. Consequently, the fact that Ball had bought from an innocent purchaser is more important than the fact that Ball had heard rumors of the fraud. Costello should not be able to impair Holliday's ability to sell the horse by giving general publicity to the fraud or spreading rumors. Moreover, it would hamper trade if a potential buyer bore the burden of checking out every rumor of a defect in the title of personal property, running back perhaps many years. Again, Costello is in a better position than Ball or Holliday to protect himself against fraud; on balance, Ball and Holliday stand in greater need of the law's protection.

A judge writing on a clean slate might reach the opposite result in Case 5. Ball's argument depends in substantial part on the presumption that Case 3 was decided correctly for Holliday. The legal community's practice of stare decisis, however, supports the presumption that Ball should be treated like Holliday if her case is more like Holliday's than it is like Abbott's in Case 2. The law could easily have evolved differently. But, having evolved as it did, a change is unlikely unless underlying social circumstances change or notions of justice mutate.

To review, the decision in each common law case elaborates on the legal experience (absent overruling). A judgment of importance should not be made ad hoc: It should flow from the principles and policies embedded in the precedents, according to the conventions of the profession. Each decision is creative to the extent that each problem case presents a new question. So the law's purposes should be elaborated as necessary to justify the decision and its forebears as members of a family—to show how the decisions are consistent with each other and may contribute to a more orderly and just society.

2. Purposes in Statutes

To illustrate the play of purpose in statutory cases, recall that the principle of legislative supremacy generally requires judges to subordinate their personal views to the enacted views of the people's representatives in the legislature. The rules enacted by legislatures, however, do not dictate the conclusion in a case entirely by deduction. A judgment of importance is required to place a problem case in a class of cases designated by an enacted rule. The statute's purposes help make the judgment of importance here, similarly to the common law.

Recall the case of Franny Farmer and Morris Auster in Chapter 3. Farmer reneged on a deal to sell peaches to Auster. Auster wanted to sue Farmer to enforce the contract. Section 2-201(1) of the Uniform Commercial Code stood as a possible barrier to Auster's action. It provided that, to be enforceable, a class of contracts for the sale of goods must be in writing and signed by the party to be charged (Farmer). The Auster/Farmer contract was oral. Auster's prospects in court consequently depended on an exception to §2-201(1), set forth in §2-201(2). This exception might allow a court to enforce the Auster/Farmer contract because Auster sent Farmer a confirmatory letter to remind her of their deal, and she did not object. This would be so, however, only if the contract was "between merchants"—if both parties were "chargeable with the knowledge or skill of merchants" (§2-104(3)). Though it is clear that Auster is chargeable as a "merchant," it is not at all clear that Farmer is chargeable as one for the purposes of this case. A judgment of importance is necessary to determine which of the facts in the case will or should lead a judge to decide whether the Auster/Farmer contract was "between merchants."

A judge in Auster's case should decide whether the law's purposes are better implemented by requiring Auster to put such deals in writing or by requiring Farmer to object to confirmatory letters. The judge, however, is unlikely to judge importance in

Auster's case apart from the legal experience. Principles of constitutional democracy and legislative supremacy are deeply ingrained in our legal culture. What matters is what the legislature was trying to do in Article 2 of the Uniform Commercial Code and, specifically, in §2-201 and the relevant definitional provisions.

Given a general background in the law of sales contracts, the legislature's purposes can be discerned from the statutory text together with its context. A judge in Auster's case should show how a decision can be reconciled with the statutory materials so that Auster is not required to act differently from how *anyone* should act in the same circumstances. The judgment of importance in Auster's case will flow from the principles and policies embedded in the legal experience, elaborated as necessary to justify the decision and in a way that implements the statutory scheme.

A central policy of the law of sales contracts encourages people to promise to buy and sell goods, such as the projected exchange of peaches for money between Auster and Farmer. Exchange benefits society because trade contributes to economic prosperity. The law assumes that people promise fewer such exchanges when they hesitate to rely on others to keep their promises. Enforcing contracts may encourage exchange by encouraging people to keep their promises. Accordingly, the law generally enforces promises to buy and sell goods.

As the requirement of a writing for enforcing a class of contracts suggests, however, the law does not enforce *all* promises to exchange goods. *Voluntary* trade contributes to economic prosperity. Consequently, the law should enforce promises that really were made and hold people to the terms of their promises as made. The writing requirement may prevent unscrupulous people from alleging promises or terms of promises falsely. The tradition, at least, holds that written contracts are less likely to be fraudulent or make a fraud easier to discover and prove. Accordingly, some contracts are enforceable only if in writing and signed by the party to be charged.

The policy of promoting exchange suggests that people should be protected by the law when they reasonably expect and probably rely on others to keep promises made as part of an exchange. The principle supporting the requirement of a writing suggests that sales contract law also protects people who allegedly made such promises from being forced to keep promises they did not make.

Note that the second standard allows some oral contracts that really were made to go unenforced. It is usually easy for the parties to put it in writing, and perhaps it is generally understood in the trades that important contracts should be in writing. On the other hand, perhaps the writing requirement should be abolished because it invalidates too many contracts in a time of telephone shopping and electronic mail; until it is abolished, however, a judge is duty-bound to work with the law in force, attributing to it the best justification that the legal community can muster.

These two purposes help to determine whether Farmer is "chargeable as a merchant" such that the Auster/Farmer contract was "between merchants" and that §2-201(2) will remove the requirement of a writing signed by Farmer so that Auster can enforce the deal. When Auster sent the letter to Farmer, reminding her of their deal, he probably expected her to reply and object if there in fact was no deal or if he got the terms wrong. Not receiving a reply, he probably relied on a belief that the deal was on and conducted himself accordingly. The purposes of this law suggest that his expectation should be protected if it was reasonable—if encouraging people like Auster to so rely would encourage exchange and without allowing the unscrupulous to stick people like Farmer with phony deals too easily.

With this background, the more specific purpose embedded in §2-201(2) can be brought to light. The statutory text says that the law would consider Auster's reliance to be reasonable only if Farmer was chargeable as a merchant, and a merchant is defined as one who "deals in goods of the kind or otherwise holds [her]self out as having knowledge or skill peculiar to the practices . . . involved in the transaction." The word *otherwise* in the definition suggests that all people who deal in goods of the kind are deemed to hold themselves out in the manner described. The more pertinent textual definition of "between merchants," requiring both parties to be "chargeable with the knowledge and skill of merchants," confirms that "deals in goods of the kind" should be interpreted this way. People who so hold themselves out—by dealing or by representations—lead others to expect and probably to rely on them to use their knowledge and skill, much as people who make promises lead others to expect and rely on them to keep their promises. In §2-201(2), then, a contract is "between merchants" if the parties, by the nature of their businesses or by representations, lead others to expect an objection if a confirmatory letter is received and is not an accurate confirmation of a real deal.

The precise question in Auster's case, then, is whether, by the nature of her business or by representations, Farmer led Auster to reasonably expect her to object to the confirmatory letter if it was inaccurate. From the facts as stated in Chapter 3, there is no reason to believe that Farmer made such representations. There are facts that characterize the nature of her business: Her orchard was described as a "small, family-run" business; she makes as few as one peach sale for a few hundred boxes in a year. These facts are important because they suggest Farmer may not be a sophisticated businessperson. On the other hand, as the UCC's official commentary suggests, almost everyone in business would be expected to answer the mail.[6] On balance, therefore, Auster's expectation seems reasonable. Farmer should have objected to protect herself from fraud. The Auster/Farmer contract should be held to be "between merchants." Section 2-201(2) applies to this transaction. And the lack of a writing signed by Farmer would not bar enforcement of the contract by Auster.

The statutory context confirms this interpretation of the text. Article 2 as a whole contains many provisions looking to ordinary business practices as a source of reasonable expectations. For example, §1-102 provides that the statute should be liberally construed and applied to promote its underlying purposes, among which are the promotion of commercial practices. Section 1-205 provides that a contract should be interpreted in light of any usage of the trade, which is defined as "any practice or method of dealing having such regularity of observance in a place, vocation or trade as to justify an expectation that it will be observed with respect to the transaction in question." Numerous provisions require the parties to sales contracts to conform to commercially reasonable practices unless otherwise agreed. Moreover, the drafting history of Article 2 and the secondary literature confirm that this statute sought generally to bring the law of sales contracts into conformity with reasonable commercial practices and expecta-

---

[6] U.C.C. §2-104, Comment 2.

tions.[7] Therefore, interpreting the definition of "between merchants" to protect reliance on reasonable commercial practices concerning confirmatory letters furthers the purposes of the law as a whole.

The statutory definitions themselves are puzzling and inadequate if applied to the facts of a case deductively, based only on the ordinary meanings of the words. As indicated in Chapter 3, contradictory conclusions are possible and of equal logical validity. Having generated a conventional justification from the text, its context, and the secondary literature, however, the problem is far less perplexing. The principle of legislative supremacy and the policies of sales contract law involving the protection of reasonable expectations and the promotion of voluntary trade reflect the legal conventions as they bear on cases like Auster's. The conventions of the legal community select from all logically possible conclusions those that implement the law's purposes. A judge may make a judgment of importance by synthesizing the legal experience in light of the legal conventions.

In sum, members of the legal community generally consider the proper judicial role to be limited by principles of stare decisis and legislative supremacy. Judges acting in good faith do not make the judgment of importance in a case in isolation. They take the common law precedents or statutory materials to be authoritative. They work, if sometimes only implicitly, with the principles and policies embedded in the legal materials, which are reliable indications of the pertinent legal conventions. The law's purposes are elaborated as necessary to decide new questions, reconciling each decision with the relevant precedents or statutory materials and, together with the legal conventions, contributing to the law's vision of a more orderly and just society.

---

[7] E.g., U.C.C. §2-104, Comments 1 & 2; Richard Danzig, A Comment on the Jurisprudence of the Uniform Commercial Code, 27 Stan. L. Rev. 621 (1975); Zipporah Batshaw Wiseman, The Limits of Vision: Karl Llewellyn and the Merchant Rules, 100 Harv. L. Rev. 465 (1987).

CHAPTER SEVEN

The Judge's Perspective

THE PRECEDING CHAPTER highlighted the law's purposes—the principles and policies that should justify legal rules and yield reasons for classifying cases within the framework of law described by the legal rules. To bring these roles out, however, I simplified matters again, though not unrealistically. In many cases, only one purpose lies behind a law or several relevant purposes have a single implication for the decision of a case. Given agreement on the facts, lawyers and judges should come to the same legal conclusion in such cases, even if they might give different explanations for so doing. In many other cases, however, competing purposes have conflicting implications. These are harder cases, in which the law is unsettled and the outcome will be uncertain, even when the facts are not in dispute.

The harder cases are more interesting, whether you seek profit, public service, or fun from lawyering. They are more likely to reach appellate judges and shape the law. The difference between harder and easier cases is one of degree. Both are capable of reasonable treatment in light of the legal conventions—what members of the legal community generally will take to be required by an orderly and just society in a case, as indicated by the legal experience and the law's purposes.

A.   Easier Cases

As a practical matter, it is not necessary to appeal explicitly to the law's purposes in easier cases. The legal rules, by their ordinary meanings, may do an adequate job of calling the important facts into prominence. Or, the purposes may converge to suggest a single result, making it superfluous to give the full argument explicitly. The role of purpose is hidden either way. However, understanding the hidden role of purpose in easier cases is helpful to understanding its more complex and explicit role in harder cases.

Imagine a simple case: Old Man Featherstone was a wealthy landowner. He had no surviving immediate family of his own, only nieces, nephews, and cousins. He also had a grandson born out of wedlock, whom he barely knew. Featherstone was thought to be a bit of a crank, and he deeply resented the frequent self-ingratiating kindnesses of his relatives. He knew they were motivated solely by greed. Following his death, the hopeful relatives gathered to hear the will read. They were shocked to find that the Old Man left his entire estate to his grandson. The will was typed in proper form, duly signed by Featherstone, and witnessed by two people whose signatures appeared.

Some of the relatives were upset enough to challenge the will. Let us assume that the estate would go to two cousins if there were no will or if the grandson had died before the Old Man. Assume also that the relevant statute (the *Statute of Wills*) provides that a person's property shall go to whomever is named in a valid will and that, to be valid, a will must be signed by the testator (Featherstone), while sane and not under fraud or duress, and in the presence of two witnesses whose signatures appear. To apply this statute, a judge would reason deductively. Thus, Featherstone's will named his grandson. It was signed by him and witnessed by two people whose signatures appeared. From the facts as stated, there is no reason to believe he was insane or a victim of fraud or duress. Therefore, the will is valid. The grandson will inherit the estate. The case is easy.

You might think that purpose has nothing to do with this case because deduction from the statute is wholly adequate.[1] So it appears. But two variations on this case will show that the law's purposes, too, justify this decision. Moreover, many easier cases can be justified adequately only with recourse to purpose. Conse-

---

[1] See Benjamin Cardozo, The Nature of the Judicial Process 112-114 (1921); Ronald Dworkin, Taking Rights Seriously 81, 337 (1978); H.L.A. Hart, Positivism and the Separation of the Law and Morals, 71 Harv. L. Rev. 593, 607-608 (1958); Neil MacCormick, Legal Reasoning and Legal Theory 100 (1978). Both Dworkin and Hart seem to have had subsequent doubts about the logic of easy cases. See Ronald Dworkin, Law as Interpretation, 60 Texas L. Rev. 527, 545 (1982); H.L.A. Hart, Problems of Philosophy in Law, in 6 Ency. Phil. 264, 271 (R. Edwards ed. 1967). See also Frederick Schauer, Easy Cases, 58 S. Calif. L. Rev. 399 (1985).

quently, deduction does not adequately justify easier cases in general.

For the first variation, imagine Featherstone left two wills. One gave the estate to two cousins; the other gave the estate to the grandson. The will favoring the grandson bore a date subsequent to the will favoring the cousins. Both wills were otherwise identical, save that the first will was witnessed by two people and the second by three.[2]

Assume the relevant statutory rules are the same as before with the addition of a rule providing that a subsequent valid will revokes a prior will. The grandson will inherit the estate only if the second will is valid; that is, if it was signed by Featherstone, while sane and not under fraud or duress, and in the presence of two witnesses whose signatures appear. Does the estate go to the cousins or the grandson? The fact of a third witness on the subsequent will is the only possibly significant problem, though it seems as clear as before that a judge should award the estate to the grandson.

You cannot justify this result by deduction from the statutory rule, which requires the will to be witnessed "by two witnesses." The statute does not say "at least two witnesses" or "at most two witnesses" or "two and only two witnesses." "Three witnesses" surely is not the same as "two witnesses." You cannot possibly deduce either that the will is valid or not valid. It is not known whether the fact of a third witness is important. A judge, too, would be puzzled if only rules, facts, and logic were considered.

The law's purposes lurk behind the easiness of this case: Why should two witnesses be required for a will to be valid? The conventions of the profession assign several purposes to such a requirement.[3] In theory, the witnessing ceremony serves to bring home to the testator the legal significance and possible finality of what he is doing; the requirement tries to assure that he acts with due deliberation. The witnesses also serve to reduce the likelihood of some person fabricating a will for another, on the assumption that it is harder to get two people to witness a fraudulent docu-

---

[2] This illustration is adapted from William R. Bishin & Christopher D. Stone, Law, Language and Ethics 724-726 (1972).

[3] See generally Ashbel G. Gulliver & Catherine J. Tilson, Classification of Gratuitous Transfers, 51 Yale L.J. 1, 5-15 (1941).

ment and escape detection. (Perhaps one witness will not do because that person could be the perpetrator of the fraud.) And the witnesses might later provide evidence of the testator's mental health when he signed his will and of other circumstances at the signing. (Perhaps one witness will not do because of the greater risk that that person will be unavailable should a dispute arise years later.) Because three witnesses serve all of these purposes better than two witnesses, there is no reason for the third signature to invalidate the subsequent will.

This conventional justification of the second case underlies the first case along with the previous justification. Two witnesses serve adequately to assure due deliberation by the testator, to reduce the likelihood of fraud, and to provide evidence of the circumstances at the signing, as determined authoritatively by the legislature. Whatever purposes the statute might serve, they have a single implication in the first case. A judge should decide that that will is valid (in this respect) because of both deduction and, implicitly, the statute's purposes.

The first case can be justified by both deduction and purpose, but the second can be justified only by looking to underlying purposes. Now consider another variation. The facts are similar to the first case except that the will leaving the estate to the grandson was not witnessed but was in Featherstone's handwriting and was signed by him. (Such a will is called a *holographic will*.) Assume that, the preceding year, the highest appellate court in the relevant jurisdiction held that a holographic will executed by some other testator was valid even though not witnessed. A judge should decide the third case of Old Man Featherstone's will the same way. This, too, is an easier case.

Like the second case, you cannot justify this one by deduction from the statute of wills. Nor can you justify it sufficiently by analogy from the precedent without calling on the law's purposes to make the judgment of importance.[4] The third case differs from the preceding cases because the plausible purposes generate reasonable arguments for the cousins and the grandson.

The absence of a witnessing ceremony might weaken the law's effort to assure due deliberation by the testator and to provide

---

[4] The hypothetical assumes the precedent is based on the common law.

evidence of the circumstances at the signing. But the fact that the will was in Featherstone's handwriting tends to indicate some deliberation (as contrasted with an oral will) and to reduce the possibility of frauds that could not be detected by handwriting experts. Whether the fact of no witnesses or the fact of a handwritten will is more important under the circumstances depends on how the reasons stemming from these now-competing purposes are weighed.

This could be a harder case. The preceding year, however, the court in the precedent was presented with this very question under similar circumstances. By holding that the holographic will in that case was valid, the court resolved the conflict in favor of the grandson's position. Consequently, a judge should decide that the third will is valid in this jurisdiction because the recent decision is stare decisis—a thing decided. The case is easier because the purposes, as weighed to decide the recent precedent, point to one outcome.

We have examined three easier cases. Deduction justifies only one, but the conventionally understood purposes of the law justify all three. Each represents a kind of case that will be found in the legal world. We can conclude, then, that easier cases in general are better justified by the law's purposes, whether or not they are made explicit.

The singular implication of the relevant purposes makes easier cases easier. This implication may result in two ways: In the first two cases, all relevant purposes pointed in the same direction; in the third, the purposes pointed in different directions, but a recent precedent resolved the competition. As a practical matter, given the precedent and stare decisis, the relevant purposes had one implication in that case as well.

B.   A Harder Case

Of course, the relevant purposes in a case can have multiple and competing implications for judicial decision. Purposes may conflict in ways not resolved by the precedents and enactments, as they had been in the third case of Old Man Featherstone's will. Or a previously unaccepted but plausible purpose may compete for acceptance as a new convention against a traditionally accepted purpose. In either situation, both sides in such cases will have reasonable arguments. The judgment of importance in such cases is harder.

Consider a fourth variation.[5] Old Man Featherstone informed his cousins and grandson that his estate would go to the grandson under a duly executed will. Some weeks later, Featherstone discovered that his grandson had concealed his heavy debts due to a gambling obsession. Featherstone confronted his grandson, who told the Old Man to mind his own business. Featherstone threatened to disinherit his grandson who, in response, drew a knife and stabbed Featherstone to death. The grandson was convicted of murder in a criminal court and sentenced to fifteen years in prison. The cousins challenge the will in court because they do not think a man's murderer should inherit his property.

Assume that the relevant statutory law provides that a person's estate shall pass upon death to the person or persons named in a valid written will. Assume also that Old Man Featherstone's will was in writing and was valid, that no statutory or other enacted rule denies the right of a murderer to inherit from his victim, and that the cousins clearly would inherit the estate if there were no will or if the grandson had died before the Old Man. It might appear that the law gives Old Man Featherstone's estate to his grandson. But this deduction is troubling; most of us probably think it *should* matter that the grandson murdered Featherstone to prevent him from changing the will. A judge's problem is to show that *the law* precludes the grandson from taking the estate because that fact is legally important.

The statute's purposes in this case indicate that both sides have plausible legal arguments. The grandson's lawyer can argue that the principle of legislative supremacy requires the court to follow the law exactly as laid down by the legislature. It would promote disorder for the court to guess what the legislature might think about a case it had not thought about. The purpose of the statute is revealed best by its terms, taken literally. The law thus gives the estate to the person named in a valid will—in this case the grandson. This result gives effect to the revealed intention of the testator

---

[5] This illustration is adapted from the famous case of Riggs v. Palmer, 106 N.Y. 506 (1889).

and avoids any need to guess the intentions of a dead man. Sticking to the written document promotes the orderly passing of property from one generation to another. Therefore, this argument concludes, the legislature should change the law if it needs to be changed.

On the other hand, the lawyer for the cousins can argue that the underlying purpose of the law is to provide for the orderly and just passing of property from one generation to the next according to the testator's desire. In normal circumstances, giving the estate to those named in the will furthers this purpose well. This, however, is an unusual case in which following the literal meaning of the will does not further the law's purposes. No reasonable testator could want his estate to go to his murderer, and no reasonable legislature could have intended such a result. Moreover, justice would not be promoted by allowing one to inherit after murdering the testator to prevent a change in a will. A basic principle of the law is that no person shall profit by his own wrong. Therefore, it is important that the grandson murdered the Old Man. The statute, this argument concludes, does not require the grandson to inherit the estate.

This is a harder case due to multiple purposes with competing implications. The grandson's argument places greater stress on the *orderly* passing of property from one generation to the next. It emphasizes the literal interpretation of the statutory text, the clarity of the testator's written will, and the uncertainty of guessing a dead man's intention. That the grandson murdered the testator is not important for this purpose. By contrast, the cousins' argument stresses the *just* passing of property from one generation to the next. It emphasizes the unusual circumstances, the probable intention of the testator and the legislature, and the injustice of rewarding wrongful behavior. The fact that the grandson murdered the testator to prevent a change in the will is important for this purpose.

The competing purposes in this case all are embedded in the legal experience, generating legal reasons with weight. A judge should decide which are the stronger under the circumstances. Parenthetically, note that harder cases also occur when the implications of embedded purposes differ from the implications of a plausible principle or policy that perhaps should back the law but has yet to enjoy conventional acceptance within the legal community. The latter kind of purpose may have some support among members of the legal community and be articulated in appellate briefs, concurring and dissenting judicial opinions, or the secondary literature. A case that accepts such a purpose and is decided according to its implications is likely a "landmark" decision, which will overrule established precedents, thereby changing the law. Judges in such cases exercise a special lawmaking power that is not only a matter of legal reasoning. Our attention here focuses on cases in which legal reasoning is dominant.

C.   Deciding Harder Cases

We have seen that easier cases in general are easier due to the single implication of the relevant purposes in the case; harder cases are hard due to the conflicting implications of competing purposes in the case. The next question concerns how the judgment of importance is made in harder cases.

1.   Webs of Belief

Judicial reasoning is but a stylized and rigorous version of the reasoning used in everyday life. Beneath the dignified bearing, the black robes, and the air of mystical capacity, judges are human beings who think basically as you and I do. Much depends on judgment, though professional legal judgments are influenced by legal education, developed by experience, and refined in each case through legal research, reflection, and argument within the legal conventions. Something useful can be said about legal reasoning and judgment in harder cases if we first consider human reasoning and judgment in simple everyday problem situations.

Imagine you and a fellow birdwatcher are walking one afternoon along a path in a park when your friend calls attention to a bird in a tree. She asks what kind of bird it is, and you say, "I believe it is a crow." But your friend says she thinks it is a blackbird. You argue for a bit, during which you say that you believe yourself to be an expert birdwatcher and that you care and understand about these things. The disagreement is left unresolved. That evening, you pick up a copy of the Audubon Society magazine, which you believe to be careful and expert about birds. You find a picture of a bird you think is the same kind as the bird in the park. The caption, to your relief, says "Crow." You feel confirmed in the opinion ventured earlier and believe you were correct.

By contrast, imagine the caption below the picture in the magazine had said "Blackbird." Depending on how serious a birdwatcher you are, you might feel disappointed. In the first situation, all of your beliefs together had a single implication under the circumstances. You could believe that it was a crow in the park, and that you are an expert bird watcher, that the Audubon Society magazine is careful and expert about birds, that the bird in the picture is of the same kind as the bird in the park, and also that you care and understand about these things. In the second situation, however, your beliefs have conflicting implications under the circumstances. Something must give.

You have several alternatives. You can maintain that the bird in the park was a crow if you drop the belief either that the Audubon Society magazine is careful and expert about birds or that the bird in the picture is the same kind as the bird in the park. Or you can decide that the bird in the park was really a blackbird, as long as you drop the belief that you are an expert birdwatcher. Or you can decide that it all makes very little sense, if you drop the belief that you care and understand about these things. However, you cannot maintain that the bird in the park was a crow and, at the same time, hold unmodified all of the beliefs you held before seeing the bird in the picture with its caption.

The beliefs bearing on this matter are like a web in which each relevant belief is connected with several others that, in turn, are connected with many of the beliefs that you hold. The web is a "seamless web" because no one belief is the starting point from which all others necessarily follow. Each belief is supported by a complex network in which all, ultimately, are mutually reinforcing in light of experience. A change in any one belief has a ripple effect causing changes in a number of other beliefs. Any belief can be changed without producing a tattered web if consequential changes are made.

Accordingly, which alternative you select in the second situation will be a function of many, if not all, of your beliefs about yourself and the way the world works. It would be easier for me, for example, to give up the belief I foolishly held that I am an expert birdwatcher. I can quickly concede that the Audubon Society is more likely to get it right than I am. Also, I would not have noticed enough about the bird in the park to be sure it was not the same kind as the bird in the picture. I want things to make sense, so I would conclude that the bird in the park probably was a blackbird.

My friend Judy, however, happens to be a professor of ornithology. Under the same circumstances, she would find it harder to give up her belief that she is an expert birdwatcher, easier to challenge the accuracy of the Audubon Society magazine, and harder to conclude that her initial belief that the two birds were of the same kind was wrong. She, too, wants these things to make sense. So she might conclude that the magazine had made an error. My other friend, Clarence, thinks of himself as an expert in everything and finds it hard ever to admit an error, most of all to himself. He also is proud to serve on the Audubon Society's board of directors. Perhaps he is more likely to conclude that the bird in the park was not the same kind as the bird in the picture. And my friend Albert, who is not very smart, is quite accustomed to confusion. Perhaps he is more likely to hold contradictory beliefs in this situation and, with a shrug, drop his belief that he cares and understands about these things.

Logically speaking, anyone could select any alternative in these circumstances if he were willing to adjust his web of beliefs as necessary to accommodate the alternative selected.[6] Psychologically speaking, however, each of us is likely to select the alternative requiring the fewest adjustments to maintain the coherence of our webs of beliefs.[7] Moreover, we try to conserve those beliefs that are most likely to work well given what we are trying to do—those beliefs that, if acted on, have not and likely will not produce disappointing experiences given our purposes. (Of course, there is no guarantee that operating this way will provide us with all and only true beliefs.)

---

[6] See generally Willard Van Orman Quine & J. G. Ullian, The Web of Beliefs (1970); Willard Van Orman Quine, Two Dogmas of Empiricism, in From a Logical Point of View 20 (W. Quine ed. 1961).

[7] Leon Festinger, A Theory of Cognitive Dissonance (1957).

Accordingly, I am likely to conclude that the bird in the park was probably a blackbird, though maintaining that it is a crow is as possible logically. I hold my beliefs about my birdwatching skills lightly and can give them up easily; I am too inexperienced to be attached to them. I hold my beliefs about the reliability of reputations of groups like the Audubon Society more deeply. I would much prefer to alter my belief about my birdwatching skills, which requires me to alter very few other beliefs that I depend on, than to alter my beliefs about the reputation of the Audubon Society. In the way I manage my general web of beliefs, I think I am like other people. Judges, too, are people; they just have distinctive experiences and goals.

2. Webs of Belief About Law

The birdwatcher situations are comparable to easier and harder cases. The first birdwatcher situation is like easier cases because all relevant beliefs, like the purposes in the first cases of Old Man Featherstone's will, converge to suggest a single result. Harder cases are like the second birdwatcher situation because a number of relevant beliefs, like the purposes in the fourth case of Old Man Featherstone's will, have conflicting implications. However, the judicial response to a harder case should be more constrained than a layperson's response in a situation of conflict. Among a judge's core beliefs should be those concerning judicial responsibility: The judge is under a duty to uphold the law, not to decide according to personal views which are not coincident with the law. Therefore, a judge's decision should be accommodated coherently with a deep commitment to the rule of law and all that this ideal entails.

Before being confronted with the facts of a harder case, the judge holds a web of beliefs about law. For example, the judge in the fourth case of Old Man Featherstone's will (in which the grandson murdered the Old Man) probably would include among the law's purposes that the law in such circumstances should provide for the orderly and just passing of property from one generation to the next; that the law should give effect to the revealed intention of the testator and avoid guessing a dead man's intentions; that the courts should follow the law as laid down by the legislature; that following the literal meaning of the will does not always serve the law's purposes; that no reasonable testator could want his estate to go to his murderer; that no reasonable legislature could have intended such a result; and that a basic principle requires that no person should profit by his own wrong. The previously decided cases might be reconciled coherently under all of these principles and policies. On being confronted with the problem case, however, the judge becomes aware of competition among purposes. The law's coherence seems to fall apart.

Such an experience may lead the judge to review her web of beliefs about the law to determine which parts should be adjusted to accommodate a decision in the case as coherently as possible. Logically speaking, the judge can conclude either that the grandson should inherit or not inherit if she is willing to make the necessary adjustments to her beliefs about law. Like a layperson, the judge will select from among the logical possibilities those that can be reconciled with past experience in light of relevant purposes. But the layperson considers a belief to work well if it comports with *his* past experiences and probably will not lead to future disappointing experiences *to him* in light of *his* personal goals. By contrast, a judge is a professional with serious obligations to serve the community. She should consider a belief to work well if it comports with *the legal community's* past experiences and will not lead to disappointing experiences *for the legal community*. She will try to make the fewest adjustments necessary to accommodate a decision coherently with the precedents and legislative materials in light of the legal community's conventional justifications for what has gone before.

To elaborate, on taking the oath of office in good faith, a judge assumes a duty to support the rule of law, which requires regular and coordinated action among legal officials. The judge's web of beliefs about law consequently should include the law's conventional justifications, which are crucial for regularity and coordination. Order and justice should be at the center, where they can support the remainder of the web, which should work out the implications of those values for legal precedents, rules, principles, and policies. To have value in pursuing order and justice, a legal web of beliefs should synthesize the legal experience and the law's purposes as a coherent and valuable whole. The principles and policies that give coherence to the rules and precedents should be those accepted by the legal community as conventional justifications for the laws. The conscientious judge faced with a harder case should reach the decision that requires the fewest adjustments to maintain or enhance the coherence of the law, given the centrality of order and justice. Accordingly, a judge should prefer to abandon or modify those beliefs about law that deviate more from the conventions of the legal community.

The judicial opinion in the case of *Riggs v. Palmer*,[8] from which the harder case of Old Man Featherstone's will is adapted, illustrates well the operation of this conventional perspective on legal reasoning. Not surprisingly, the New York Court of Appeals held that a person who murders a testator to prevent the testator from changing his will may not inherit property under the will, notwithstanding a statute of the kind described above. The interesting part is the court's reasoning in support of this conclusion.

After stating the facts in that case, Judge Robert Earl, writing for the court, noted the grandson's argument that the will was made in proper form and must have effect according to the letter of the law. He conceded that the relevant statutes, if literally construed, gave the property to the murderer. He then embarked on an extensive discussion of the principle of legislative supremacy.

Judge Earl abandoned the view that the principle of legislative supremacy requires statutes to be interpreted literally in all cases, if he ever had held it among his beliefs about law. He retained the view that statutes should be interpreted to give effect to the legislature's intention. He thus maintained the principle of legislative supremacy, which is basic in a democratic political system, by recognizing one version of it and rejecting another.

Further, Judge Earl explained in effect, the rejected version of legislative supremacy is not generally supported by the conventions of the legal community. He quoted extensively from eminent legal writers on statutory law:

> It is a familiar canon of construction that a thing which is within the intention of the makers of a statute is as much within the

---

[8] 115 N.Y. 506 (1889).

statute as if it were within the letter; and a thing which is within the letter of the statute is not within the statute, unless it be within the intention of the makers. The writers of laws do not always express their intention perfectly, but either exceed it or fall short of it, so that judges are to collect it from probable or rational conjectures only, and this is called rational interpretation. . . . [9]

Judge Earl cited or quoted from no fewer than five legal treatises to this effect, evidencing the legal community's attitude. He also reported two proverbial cases that exemplify the operation of this view of statutory interpretation:

There was a statute in Bologna that whoever drew blood [i.e., engaged in sword-play] in the streets should be severely punished, and yet it was held not to apply to the case of a barber [i.e., a surgeon] who opened a vein in the street. It is commanded in the Decalogue that no work shall be done upon the sabbath, and yet, giving the command a rational interpretation founded upon its design, the Infallible Judge held that it did not prohibit works of necessity, charity or benevolence on that day.[10]

In light of such authority, Judge Earl was arguing, it is hard to believe that many lawyers and judges reasonably expect judges to follow statutes literally in all cases. Abandoning that version of the principle of legislative supremacy would not be greatly incompatible with the practices and dispositions of the legal community.

This left it necessary for him to determine what the legislature intended in the circumstances of this case and like cases. The thought that the legislature might have intended the murderer to inherit under his victim's will did not fit well within Judge Earl's web of beliefs about law:

What could be more unreasonable than to suppose that it was the legislative intention in the general laws passed for the orderly, peaceable and just devolution of property, that they should have operation in favor of one who murdered his ancestor that he

---

[9] Id. at 509.
[10] Id. at 511.

might speedily come into the possession of his estate? Such an intention is *inconceivable*.[11]

Moreover, Judge Earl argued, application of a certain maxim of the common law (a kind of general principle) was relevant to the "orderly, peaceable and just devolution of property":

> No one shall be permitted to profit by his own fraud, or to take advantage of his own wrong, or to found any claim upon his own inequity, or to acquire property by his own crime. These maxims are dictated by public policy, have their foundation in universal law administered in all civilized countries, and have nowhere been superseded by statutes.[12]

To illustrate, he gave a number of analogous cases exemplifying application of the maxim. In one, it was held that a person could not collect under an insurance policy according to its literal terms when he murdered the insured to make the benefits payable.[13] Justice Stephen J. Field in that case had written for the Supreme Court:

> It would be a reproach to the jurisprudence of the country, if one could recover insurance money payable on the death of a party whose life he had feloniously taken. As well might he recover insurance money upon a building that he had willfully fired.[14]

In other cases, Judge Earl reported, the courts held without statutory basis that a will would be set aside if procured by the fraud or undue influence of the person in whose favor it would operate.[15] Here, the effect of Judge Earl's argument is to suggest by analogies that members of the legal community generally are disposed to apply the principle about not allowing a person to

---

[11] Riggs v. Palmer, 115 N.Y. 506, 511 (1889) (emphasis added).

[12] Id. at 511-512. Judge Earl cited four treatises on foreign law to support his assertion that the maxim has its foundation in "universal law administered in all civilized nations."

[13] N.Y. Mut. Life Ins. Co. v. Armstrong, 117 U.S. 591 (1886).

[14] Id. at 600.

[15] Riggs v. Palmer, 115 N.Y. 506, 512 (1889) (citing two cases).

profit from his own wrong even in the face of the literal terms of an applicable statute and will.

Judge Earl's difficulty in accommodating a decision for the grandson with the legal experience, including the law's commitment to the above-quoted maxim and the presumed wisdom of the cited precedents, is further revealed by a number of hypothetical cases he posed in the analogical form:

> Here there was no certainty that this murderer would survive the testator, or that the testator would not change his will, and there was no certainty that he would get this property if nature was allowed to take its course. . . . If he had met the testator, and taken his property by force, he would have had no title to it. Shall he acquire title by murdering him? If he had gone to the testator's house, and by force compelled him, or by fraud or undue influence had induced him to will him his property, the law would not allow him to hold it. But can he give effect and operation to a will by murder, and yet take the property? To answer these questions in the affirmative, it seems to me would be a reproach to the jurisprudence of our state, and an offense against public policy.[16]

Thus, the grandson's argument depended on the view that the principle of legislative supremacy requires a literal interpretation of a statute in all cases. That view, however, conflicted with one focusing on the probable intention of the legislature and the principle reflected in the maxim. More important, it cannot be reconciled with the many real and hypothetical cases Judge Earl discussed. In his opinion, it seems, the policy of literal statutory interpretation does not work well; if recognized, it would cast doubt on much of the legal experience, displace a larger number of accepted legal conventions, and lead to disappointing experiences for the legal community. His citations to legal writers and cases support his belief that this purpose is not thought to contribute much to a more orderly and just society in this case and like cases.

Judge Earl had less difficulty accommodating a decision for the other relatives. In his opinion, it seems, the policy of "rational

---

[16] Id. at 512-513.

interpretation" and the maxim are more strongly supported by the legal community in similar circumstances, as evidenced by the many cases he discussed. Retaining these principles and policies, and therefore deciding for the other relatives, conserves the conventions that work well. So deciding maintains greater coherence in the law in its entirety than the available alternative, which injects an absurdity. Accordingly, a decision for the relatives was thought better to contribute to the orderly and just passing of property from one generation to the next, where the implications of order and justice were a function of the conventions of the legal community.[17]

To be clear, there was nothing inevitable about the result in *Riggs v. Palmer*. It was as possible logically for Judge Earl to retain the policy requiring a literal interpretation of statutes and to hold for the grandson. If it were not, the case probably would not have been litigated to the highest court in New York. Moreover, my point here is not that literal interpretation has no place in law and legal reasoning. Rather, literal interpretation is not required by the nature of law or judging. Literal interpretation, and other kinds of interpretation, should be employed when they better further the law's purposes in the relevant context. This is not always the case.

In sum, legal reasoning in law cases is complex. We have

---

[17] This approach to easier and harder cases is comparable to Professor Dworkin's early approach to hard cases. See Ronald Dworkin, Taking Rights Seriously 81-131 (1978). Dworkin would have judges in hard cases follow principles that figure in the "best" justification of the legal experience, where the "best" justification is a grand theory that (1) fits a substantial part of the legal experience and (2) is most justifiable in political morality even if less consistent with the legal experience than an alternative theory. Ronald Dworkin, Law's Empire (1986). The approach in this book emphasizes the judge's responsibility to the legal community's conventions of argument and judgment. This approach, unlike Dworkin's, does not claim that there is a "single right answer" in hard cases. It requires judges to coordinate their decisions by conforming to the conventions of the legal profession (including conventional principles and policies), rather than abstract political morality. When the conventions break down due to controversy, judges must make a little law to settle the dispute. Judges should do so, however, in an effort to win the support of the legal community by building on convention, not by acting alone and without coordination to reach a right answer as a matter of abstract morality or idiosyncrasy.

travelled far from the simple versions of deductive and analogical reasoning that give legal reasoning its form of expression. A judge need not decide a case by confronting the facts with a single rule or precedent in mind or with wholly personal value preferences, either way producing arbitrary decisions too often. A judge should judge importance according to which decision requires the least adjustment to accommodate the decision coherently with the facts of the case and the legal experience, interpreted in accordance with legal principles and policies, and supported by conventions of the legal community.

CHAPTER EIGHT

The Lawyer's Perspective

ONCE YOU VIEW THE judicial decision in harder cases as suggested in the preceding chapters, we can pose a number of entirely practical questions: How does a judge cope with the huge mass of information within the legal materials? How do lawyers develop a case and influence which decision a judge will settle on as the best? How do the analogical and deductive forms of legal reasoning work in legal advocacy? In this chapter, I will use these questions to probe the practical implications of conventional legal reasoning. I hope you will see that the lawyers play a key role in presenting a case to a court so the judges are faced with a manageable problem. Consequently, capable lawyers can have a substantial influence over the way in which a judge will approach a case, including whether it will be perceived as easier or harder. I also hope you will see that the forms of legal reasoning, together with the law's purposes and the legal conventions, can help you make reasonably reliable predictions and effective legal arguments, even in many harder problem cases.

A.   How Judges Get Started

In principle, the entire law is involved in each judicial decision. The analogical and deductive forms themselves imply a need to consider the entire law. Sound analogies not only require judges to decide each problem case as like cases have been decided; in principle, they also should distinguish each case from all other cases that might require a different result. Sound syllogisms not only require judges to decide each case by deduction from a rule of law; in principle, they should be sure that all rules requiring a different result are not applicable. This does not change when we take a broader view of the resources available for legal reasoning. We then try to accommodate a decision coherently with the facts of the case and the legal experience, interpreted in accordance with legal principles and policies, supported by conventions of the legal community. This, too, involves the entire law.

In practice, however, no one can negate the possible implications of all other cases and rules exhaustively. Nor can anyone knowingly accommodate each decision with the whole of the law. Consequently, suggesting that judges decide harder cases in accordance with the law in its entirety may seem a truism with no practical implications. It may seem to enjoin you to think about everything before doing anything—effectively ensuring that you will do nothing. The extent of the law is surely vast. You would be disabled from acting if you had to view and digest the entire law before giving advice in any case. To make law and legal reasoning manageable, you must select from the whole law those parts that are most germane to a particular case.

Law and legal reasoning should be understood as they are used in their real-world contexts, not only in the abstract as a philosophical matter. In context, they are not so overwhelming. Lawyers in fact make their predictions and arguments in light of what a judge will or should do *in a case*. Judges in fact make their decisions *in cases* that have materialized. The courts' procedural rules limit how a case can be brought to a court and how lawyers must present the case. The context set by the case refines the focus of legal reasoning for each judicial decision.

For example, a civil lawsuit is initiated when the plaintiff files a complaint with a court. In the federal courts and many state courts, a complaint must include "a short and plain statement of the claim showing that the [plaintiff] is entitled to relief," together with a request for relief, such as the payment of money by the defendant.[1] The defendant then is required to respond in one of several ways. Among them is a defendant's right to ask the court to decide that the plaintiff's complaint "fail[s] to state a claim upon which relief may be granted."[2] If the court so decides, the plaintiff's complaint is dismissed and the lawsuit ends immediately; otherwise, the parties proceed to the next step in litigation. A court will dismiss a complaint on this ground if, for example, it does not

---

[1] Fed. R. Civ. P. 8(a).
[2] Fed. R. Civ. P. 12(b)(6).

provide sufficient information to give the defendant's lawyer a reasonable idea of what facts and law might sustain the plaintiff's lawsuit. Otherwise, the defendant would not have a fair opportunity to prepare a defense.

Accordingly, bringing a case to court requires the plaintiff's lawyer to announce at the outset, albeit in a truncated way, the legal basis of the plaintiff's claim. In effect, the plaintiff's lawyer must point to a part of the legal experience and assert that that part entitles the plaintiff to the requested relief. At this early stage of litigation, the complaint need not set forth a detailed legal argument or even cite precedents and legal rules. The complaint needs to inform the court and the defendant of the facts pointing to a general area of law that might allow the plaintiff to prevail as claimed. A complaint that gestures at the law as an entirety without alleging facts constituting a cognizable legal claim would be dismissed for failing to state a claim upon which relief may be granted.

To illustrate, consider a case involving a property owner in the role of defendant and a trespasser in the role of plaintiff.[3] The property involved was an unoccupied farmhouse containing personal property. Over a ten-year period, unknown persons had broken into the farmhouse and damaged it. They took some of the defendant's possessions. The defendant then set up a booby trap, involving a shotgun, in the bedroom. The plaintiff was shot and seriously wounded in the lower leg after entering the house and opening the door to the bedroom. The plaintiff had pleaded guilty to a minor criminal trespass charge, and he then brought a civil action against the defendant for damages involving personal injuries, medical expenses, and loss of earnings occasioned by the shotgun wound. Other facts will appear below.

A lawyer for the plaintiff might file a complaint in proper form as follows:

---

[3] The illustration is based on Katko v. Briney, 183 N.W.2d 657 (Iowa 1971).

IN THE DISTRICT COURT
OF THE STATE OF WILLARD
IN AND FOR LUDWIG COUNTY

Terry Tress,	
Plaintiff	COMPLAINT
v.	Civil No. 95-1949
Oscar Olner,	Trial by Jury Demanded
Defendant	

The plaintiff, Terry Tress, states for his complaint against defendant, Oscar Olner, as follows:

1. On or about July 16, 1995, plaintiff, Terry Tress, was shot by a spring gun trap set by defendant, Oscar Olner, in an unoccupied house owned by the defendant.

2. Defendant, Oscar Olner, erected the spring gun trap with an intention to cause death or serious bodily injury to people entering the premises.

3. Defendant was not privileged to use deadly force or to erect the spring gun trap.

4. As a direct and proximate cause of the defendant's wrongful acts, plaintiff Terry Tress's leg was seriously injured, and plaintiff was prevented from working for some time, suffered great pain of body and mind, and incurred expenses for medical attention and hospitalization in the sum of forty-two thousand, seven hundred, and twenty dollars ($42,720).

WHEREFORE plaintiff, Terry Tress, demands judgment against defendant, Oscar Olner, in the sum of forty-two thousand, seven hundred, and twenty dollars ($42,720) plus interest from the date the cause of action arose together with his costs and expenses of prosecuting this action.

In most jurisdictions, this complaint states a claim upon which relief may be granted. By its allegations, it effectively invokes certain well-known rules and precedents in the common law of torts. All common law jurisdictions recognize a claim for battery, which occurs when one person intentionally causes harmful or offensive physical contact to the person of another without excuse or justification. If the defendant's lawyer were to ask the court to dismiss the complaint for failing to state a claim upon which relief may be granted, the plaintiff's lawyer could cite the common law rules and precedents in a brief in opposition to the defendant's request.

Only then would the judge be in a position to decide the question. She would not, however, have to think about everything before doing anything. The complaint and the rules and precedents cited in the parties' briefs would be before the court. These documents would call the judge's attention to parts of the legal experience that, in the lawyers' opinions, are relevant to the case. The judge's reasoning would focus on the cited rules and precedents, though she could draw as well on her own research and general knowledge concerning the law of torts and related criminal or property law, theories of compensation and responsibility, rules and theories of civil procedure, and other aspects of the law. Her decision would be manageable because the lawyers will have presented the case in a manner that poses a discrete question and proposes a reasoned decision.

In this respect, the judicial decision on a defendant's request to dismiss a complaint for failure to state a claim upon which relief may be granted is typical of almost all judicial decisions. Such decisions are made in a context with structure. Courts generally act in concrete cases at the specific request of a party. The request must pose a specific legal issue. The possible requests that a party can make are fixed in advance by the procedural forms. Each party is afforded an opportunity to present arguments that will call attention to relevant aspects of the legal experience. The lawyers thus take the initiative to bring into prominence the most relevant aspects of the law in its entirety, leaving the rest in the background as the context for thought.

B.   How Lawyers Get Started

The lawyers start the ball rolling for the judges, but no one similarly starts the ball rolling for the lawyers. Clients come to the law office with an often vague (and sometimes misplaced) sense that they have been wronged. They rarely provide the lawyers with much more than a bare, often biased or misleading summary of the facts of a dispute. They may be unclear about their objectives and, in any event, rarely know whether the law permits or requires what they want to do, much less what law is relevant. The lawyer should start by developing the facts, based on legal knowledge and a capacity for bringing that knowledge to bear in a concrete dispute through legal reasoning.

Imagine, for example, that the plaintiff in the spring gun case summarized above had started an initial interview with you by asking, as a client might, whether it was "legal" for someone to booby trap an abandoned farmhouse with a gun. As a competent lawyer, you would know immediately that answering the question simply yes or no would be unwise. Your general knowledge of the law would be sufficient for you to have at least a vague idea of the kinds of precedents you would find from research. You would know that there are probably some precedents in which defendants who set traps that injured other people were convicted of crimes and others in which such defendants were acquitted; some precedents in which plaintiffs injured by traps recovered damages for battery and others where injured plaintiffs did not recover. You also would have some notion that these precedents often involved the common law rules concerning battery and a property owner's privilege to use force in self-defense or the defense of property. The client's question should call your attention to these parts of the legal experience. With a moment's reflection, you would know that you need more information before you can give reliable legal advice.

The needed additional information is of three kinds. You first need to know why the client wants to know whether it is lawful to set a spring gun. Based on the simple first question asked by the client, you do not know whether the client wants to set a trap or sue someone who set one. Second, you need to know a great deal about the facts that have led or might lead to a dispute that could come before a court. Third, you need to know much about the precedents, rules, principles, and policies that will determine what a court should do in a case in the jurisdiction where you would litigate.

The second and third kinds of information are interrelated because the law determines what facts are relevant while, at the same time, the facts determine what law is relevant. Thus, you should begin a process of (1) gathering facts to narrow the focus of legal research, (2) conducting preliminary legal research, (3) gathering more facts in light of that research, (4) conducting further legal research in light of those facts, and so on.

You could begin by questioning the client to develop a preliminary picture of the relevant facts. The hard part is knowing what questions to ask. A general knowledge of the law gained from prior study, together with skill at using the analogical and deductive forms of legal reasoning, is indispensable here. Though many lawyers ask good questions instinctively, a good question can be the product of a hypothesis concerning a possible analogical or deductive relationship between the problem case and the precedents or rules that might be found within the legal experience. That the question arises from a hypothesis bears emphasizing because, at the early stages in developing a case, any one hypothesis could easily turn out to be wrong. The initial questioning of a client is like a fishing expedition—you may have some reason to believe that you have located a good fishing spot, but you never know whether the fish will be biting.

To illustrate, consider the following imaginary transcript of part of an initial interview in the spring gun case. Notice how your impression of the case changes as the lawyer elicits more facts:

> *Client (C):* Is it legal for someone to set a trap with a gun in a farmhouse?
> *Lawyer (L):* Why do you want to know?
> *C:* I was shot by one.
> *L:* Please continue.
> *C:* I want to sue the guy who set it.
> *L:* Tell me how it happened.
> *C:* I just opened the door to the bedroom and the thing went off. It nearly blew my foot off.
> *L:* I'm sorry. Are you OK now?

C: I can walk all right. It still hurts. I was in the hospital for fifteen days. In surgery twice. They almost had to take it off.

L: You were lucky. What were you doing in the farmhouse?

C: Well, I was picking up some old jars and bottles. I'd been there before.

L: Whose farmhouse was it?

C: Turns out it belongs to a guy named Olner.

L: Did you know that before you went in?

C: No. I thought the place was abandoned.

L: Why?

C: I don't live far from there, and I've passed it lots of times. It's all boarded up, overgrown—has been for years. I didn't think I was doing anything wrong by going in and taking some things no one cared about anymore.

L: Do the police know you went in?

C: Sure. They busted me for burglary. I pleaded to a lesser charge, and they fined me fifty bucks.

L: Do you know if they charged Mr. Olner?

C: Don't know.

L: Did you see any "No Trespassing" signs before you went in?

C: No.

L: Did you see any signs warning of the trap?

C: No.

L: Did you look through the windows before going in?

C: Couldn't. They were all boarded up.

L: How did you get in?

C: I—and my friend—we tore a board off. There was no glass in the window, so it was easy.

L: Then what happened?

C: Joe, my friend, went into the kitchen to look around. I saw this chair propped under a door handle, so I got curious. I moved the chair and turned the door handle. That's when it happened. Boom.

L: That thing could have shot some kid on a lark!

C: Sure.

L: Was anyone else in the farmhouse?

C: Just Joe. He took me to the hospital.

L: Have you spoken with Mr. Olner since this happened?

C: Yeah. He came to the hospital once. Said he wanted to see the bastard who was driving him and his wife nuts. He's a nasty customer.

L: Do you have a family?

C: Wife and one kid.

L: Do you work?

C: I pumped gas at Shelly's station for four years before this happened. Couldn't work for two months. I'll start again next week.

Some of this lawyer's questions are similar to those a layperson might ask. Significantly, however, others are not. The dissimilar questions are a product of the lawyer's professional training and experience—his general knowledge of the law and skill at legal reasoning. Thus, a layperson might pass by the client's seemingly innocent comment that he was in the house to pick up some old jars and bottles. But the lawyer asks a series of questions revealing that the client was a trespasser and thief. As you will see, the precedents concerning a property owner's right to use force in defense of his property sometimes allow an owner to use greater force against a thief than a mere trespasser, though when asking the question the lawyer may hypothesize only that the law might so distinguish such cases. Similarly, a layperson might not ask whether there were any "No Trespassing" signs, signs warning of the trap or other ways for an intruder to learn of the trap before being shot. But the lawyer asks such questions because the precedents might permit Olner to use a trap to scare off intruders but not to cause them death or great bodily harm. Again, a layperson might not think to ask whether there were any people in the house other than the intruders. But the lawyer might think that the cases and rules could then allow Olner to use force lawfully in defense of people when he could not use it lawfully in defense of property only. Thus, a good lawyer will be using his skill at legal reasoning even as he conducts an initial interview with a client.

After developing a preliminary account of the facts by questioning the client, you cannot yet give reliable legal advice. Except for very accomplished specialists working within an area of expertise, lawyers do not know the relevant rules and precedents in sufficient detail to give legal advice with only momentary reflection. You will have to read or reread the cases, statutes, and legal commentaries with the problem case in mind. You may be guided through this legal research by the forms of legal reasoning: The legal materials are organized in a deductive framework described by the legal rules, and your hypotheses concerning what might be suggested by the rules and precedents can lead you through the library. Then you can develop more facts (including the other party's point of view) in light of your legal research and think hard about the case.

The general knowledge possessed by every competent lawyer, together with skill in analogical and deductive reasoning, suffices for you to get started and to develop the case to a large extent. However, such knowledge and skill are not sufficient for you to make reasonably reliable predictions or effective legal arguments. Good legal advice and good advocacy require a judgment of importance. As you will see, your skills at reasoning analogically and deductively can be supplemented by skills at using the purposes of the law.

C.   Advocacy in Harder Cases

Having developed the facts and conducted legal research, you will be in a position to decide whether to advise your client to litigate, settle, or drop the matter. Your advice should depend partly on the result you predict if you litigate, as indicated in Chapter 1.[4] Your prediction, in turn, is largely a function of how you think a judge will respond to arguments to be pressed on the court by the lawyers on each side. To be sure, the predictive goal may be aided by assessments of the psychologies and politics of the players. Legal officials are by no means immune to the influences on behavior that affect humans generally. These influences, however, are modulated to a significant extent by professional training, experience, and socialization, and by a judge's duty to uphold the law.

Hence, the legal arguments are significant. Before giving sound legal advice to your client, you should compose your best argu-

---

[4] See Chapter 1 §C.

ment and anticipate your opponent's arguments. You should gauge how a judge (and, in appropriate cases, a jury) will respond to each argument. The power of the initiative gives you a precious opportunity to wield substantial influence over a judge's first impression of the case and, consequently, the decisions she will make.

The components of the judicial decision are: (1) the facts of the problem case; (2) the legal experience, including the common law precedents and rules, and enacted texts with their contexts; and (3) the conventional understandings of the relevant law's purposes. Each of these components consists of a potentially vast array of bits of information that, in interesting cases, can be combined in a number of plausible ways. Your task as an advocate is to use these bits to compose a picture showing how a judge can accommodate a decision for your client coherently within her web of beliefs about law. You can do this by (1) calling attention to particular facts, parts of the legal experience, and principles or policies; and (2) integrating these bits of information into a coherent legal argument that supports a decision for your client.

When you mention a fact, cite a precedent or rule, or explain how a principle or policy bears on the case, you call information to the judge's attention. A conscientious judge then has an "experience" like that of the birdwatchers in the previous chapter.[5] Such a judge will feel obligated to respond to this experience in one way or another. She may decide that the information does not merit attention, as when a fact is inadequately supported by the evidence, a precedent is not authoritative, a rule is not applicable to the case, or a principle or policy is not embedded in the legal experience. Or she may accept that the bit of information matters, in which case the fact, case, rule, or purpose is there to be dealt with and cannot be ignored. Each bit of information that gains attention may support or oppose the decision you prefer. How the judge will treat the information depends on how all of the relevant bits of information are combined.

A skilled advocate can influence the integrative process, in addition to calling attention to the bits that go into the process. You can use intellectual and rhetorical skills to narrate a story that

---

[5] See Chapter 7 §C.

shows how the pieces fit together to support a decision for your client. You can often describe the information in terms that evoke various connotations or associations. You can treat a point in detail to draw out the attention paid to that point and to intensify the emotional reaction. You can place information in a broader or narrower context to affect its perceived meaning or significance. By juxtaposing one bit of information to another, you can highlight compatible or anomalous relationships. You can also criticize an adversary's argument by pointing out facts or laws that challenge the coherence of his presentation.

To illustrate, assume that the jury at a trial in the spring gun case found the defendant liable and awarded damages to the plaintiff. The defendant appealed, claiming the trial judge erred in her instruction to the jury. This instruction had said that an owner of premises is prohibited from willfully or intentionally injuring a trespasser by using force that either takes life or does great bodily injury, and that use of a spring gun or similar booby trap for the purpose of thus harming trespassers is unlawful, even if the trespasser is violating the law. It added that such a use of force would be privileged only when the trespasser was committing a felony of violence or one punishable by death, or when the trespasser was endangering human life by his act.

The arguments of the two lawyers on appeal should present the judges with a summary of facts supported by evidence in the trial record, citations to and brief summaries of the common law rules and precedents relevant to the court's decision, and an argument showing how a decision for their respective clients furthers the relevant purposes of the law. In this case, like any harder case, plural but plausible versions of the facts, the legal experience, and the law's purposes are possible. Consider, first, sketches of the statements of facts that each of the lawyers could compose, with support in the trial record[6] and without contradicting the facts stated by opposing counsel.

---

[6] All of the facts that appear below were stated as fact in the majority or dissenting opinion in Katko v. Briney, 183 N.W.2d 657 (Iowa 1971). Note that a lawyer is subject to discipline for knowingly "mak[ing] a false statement of material fact or law to a [court]." Model Rules of Professional Conduct Rule 3.3(1)(1) (1992).

The defendant's lawyer might present the facts as follows:

Oscar Olner, the defendant, testified that the farmhouse in this case belonged to his wife and had been in her family for several generations. It contained furniture and other valuable possessions, including a collection of antique jars and bottles. She frequently visited the farmhouse to enjoy the collection. The house had been broken into and vandalized repeatedly in recent years. To stop the intrusions, Mr. Olner nailed the doors and some windows shut, boarded up others, locked the doors, posted seven "No Trespassing" signs, and complained on numerous occasions to the sheriff. When all of these efforts proved futile, he placed a gun in a bedroom and wired it so that it would shoot downward and toward the door if anyone opened it. He said he first aimed it straight at the door but later, at his wife's suggestion, pointed the gun down in a way he thought would only scare an intruder. He testified that he "didn't want to injure anyone."

The plaintiff was injured while making a second visit to the defendant's farmhouse to enter unlawfully and steal Mrs. Olner's antiques. He entered by tearing a plank from a porch window and was injured when he came to a closed bedroom door, removed a chair braced under the door knob, and opened the door. This action triggered the gun. The blast went through the door and struck the plaintiff just above the right ankle.

The plaintiff's lawyer might present the facts differently:

Terry Tress, the plaintiff, was shot by the defendant because, over the preceding ten years, a number of trespassing incidents occurred at the defendant's unoccupied farmhouse. The defendants over the years boarded up the windows and doors and posted a few "No Trespassing" signs on the land. However, the nearest remaining sign was thirty-five feet from the house at the time of the incident.

On June 11, 1995, following one such trespassing incident, the defendant set a shotgun trap in the north bedroom. After cleaning and oiling his 20-gauge shotgun, the power of which he was well aware, the defendant took it to the old house where he secured it to an iron bed with the barrel pointed at the bedroom door. It was rigged with wire from the doorknob to the gun's trigger so that it would fire when the door was opened, no matter who opened it. The defendant at first pointed the gun so an intruder would be hit in the stomach but, at his wife's insistence, lowered it to hit the legs. He admitted doing so because "I was mad and tired of being tormented," though he "didn't want to injure anyone." He gave no explanation of why he used a loaded shell, set it to hit a person already in the house, and posted no effective warning. The bedroom window was covered so that no one could see the trap.

Terry Tress lived with his wife and child and worked regularly as a gasoline station attendant nearby. He had observed the old house for several years, knew it was unoccupied, and thought it was abandoned. In 1995, the area around the house was covered with high weeds. The plaintiff had been there with a friend and found several old bottles and fruit jars, which he took home. On a second trip, he and his friend entered the house through a window that was without glass. As he started to enter a bedroom, the shotgun went off, striking him in the right leg below the knee. Much of the leg, including part of the tibia, was blown away. Only with his friend's help was he taken to a hospital for emergency surgery, and he remained in the hospital for fifteen days.

These two versions of the facts leave very different impressions. The defendant's account portrays the plaintiff as a heartless burglar depriving the defendant's poor wife of her family heirlooms. The defendant appears as a vigilant, if frustrated, husband defending his wife's property from persistent and anonymous vandals. By contrast, the plaintiff's account portrays the plaintiff as a hardworking family man with an interest in collecting old jars and bottles. The defendant appears as a cold and vengeful man seeking to violently punish a stranger, whether or not that person was responsible for past intrusions. You might be tempted to characterize the difference as one involving the goodness or badness of the principal players, and this is a part of what is involved in good advocacy. But the two versions at the same time bring into prominence facts that are relevant to the *legal* issues involved.

A sketch of how the defendant's lawyer might present the legal experience follows:

> The jury should have been instructed that the plaintiff in this case could not recover if the defendant set the spring gun in his dwelling house with the intent to repel, but not seriously injure, a felonious intruder. In Scheuerman v. Sharfenberg, 163 Ala. 337 (1909), the plaintiff had been badly hurt by a spring gun while burglarizing the defendant's storehouse. The court assimilated the storehouse to a dwelling and held that the plaintiff could not recover because he was injured while committing a felony. In Hooker v. Miller, 37 Iowa 613 (1873), the court held that a plaintiff who was injured by a spring gun while trespassing in the defendant's garden could recover, but placed emphasis on the fact that the plaintiff was not committing a felony and did not trespass in a dwelling house. Many cases have held that a property owner is privileged to use reasonable force, including devices, to repel an invader even if there is no threat to human life or safety. E.g., Allison v. Fiscus, 156 Ohio 120 (1951).

The plaintiff's lawyer might present the legal experience differently:

> The trial court's instruction was correct to limit the defendant's privilege to use force to situations in which there is a threat to human life, whether or not the intruder is a wrongdoer. A property owner is privileged to use mechanical devices that inflict great bodily harm only if he

would be entitled to use such force in person. State v. Childers, 133 Ohio St. 508, 515 (1938). One person is not privileged to use deadly force or force likely to do great bodily harm to protect property, even from burglary, absent an accompanying threat to the life or safety of a person. People v. Ceballos, 12 Cal. 3d 470, 479 (1974). In Hooker v. Miller, 37 Iowa 613 (1873), the court held that a vineyard owner was liable for damages resulting from a spring shot gun although the plaintiff was a criminal trespasser and there to steal grapes. Accord, Bird v. Holbrook, 130 Eng. Rep. 911 (1825).

These two sketches also leave very different impressions.[7] The defendant's account emphasizes the precedents allowing a property owner to use force to protect his dwelling and highlights the criminal conduct of the intruder. Accordingly, the facts as stated above by the defendant's lawyer call attention to the defendant's effort to protect his property, using force only after taking a number of less aggressive measures unsuccessfully, and to the plaintiff's intention to steal valuable antiques from the farmhouse. By contrast, the plaintiff's account emphasizes the precedents limiting a property owner's privilege to use force to protect property when there is no threat to human life or safety, and giving little or no weight to the criminal conduct of the intruder. Accordingly, the facts stated above by the plaintiff's lawyer call attention to the plaintiff's reasons for believing that the farmhouse was abandoned and, without denying that the plaintiff trespassed, treat his adventure almost as a misguided lark. The defendant is portrayed as acting recklessly, without concern for the circumstances under which a person may be shot, if not with a malicious intention to seek revenge for the past intrusions by others.

---

[7] A lawyer is subject to discipline for knowingly "fail[ing] to disclose to [a court] any legal authority in the controlling jurisdiction known to the lawyer to be directly adverse to the position of the client and not disclosed by opposing counsel." Model Rules of Professional Conduct Rule 3.3(a)(3) (1992). If the spring gun case arose in Iowa, for example, both lawyers should bring the case of Hooker v. Miller to the court's attention. Note how each legal argument does so, but spins it in a way that supports the client's position.

A court consequently would be faced with two versions of the facts and the law, both of which are plausible. The defendant's version fits the facts and the legal experience together compatibly, as does the plaintiff's. The court's decision depends on which version fits better with the remainder of the legal experience and conventional understandings of the law's purposes. Surely the parties' advocates are well advised to continue their arguments to show how their versions can be coherently accommodated with the principles and policies that justify this part of the law.

The defendant's lawyer might continue along the following lines:

> There is no doubt in this case that the plaintiff was a wrongdoer—a thief who entered the defendant's dwelling house without permission. The defendant acted in defense of his valuable property after taking a large number of nonviolent measures unsuccessfully and with no wrongful intention to harm intruders unnecessarily. The common law tradition upholds the right of a homeowner to protect his dwelling by the use of force, including deadly force. W. Prosser, Handbook of the Law of Torts 116 (4th ed. 1971). "The principle that controls is that the right need never yield to wrong, where the justification of self-defense has shown the defendant to be in the right and the plaintiff in the wrong. To deny the use of deadly force necessarily allows the plaintiff to profit from his own wrong even when the defendant is able to stop him." Epstein, Intentional Harms, 4 J. Legal Stud. 391, 419 (1975) (citation omitted).

The plaintiff's lawyer of course would continue differently:

> The law has always placed a higher value on human safety than on mere rights in property. W. Prosser, Handbook of the Law of Torts 115 (4th ed. 1971). Consequently, "spring guns and other man-killing devices are not justifiable against a mere trespasser, or even a petty thief." Id. at 116. See also 2 F. Harper and F. James, The Law of Torts

1440-1441 (1956). It makes no difference that the plaintiff entered a farmhouse because the privilege to use greater force to defend a dwelling exists only when there is a threat to the safety of people residing therein; in this case, the farmhouse was unoccupied. See People v. Ceballos, 12 Cal. 3d 470 (1974). It makes no difference that the plaintiff was a trespasser because the foundation of the law is "not the criminality of the act or the turpitude of the trespasser." Hooker v. Miller, 37 Iowa 613, 615 (1873). The privilege of a property owner to use force against an intruder is limited to force that is proportional to the nature of the intrusion; "it would seem clear that no interest which is merely one of property can be equal or superior to the interest which both the individual and society have in life and limb." Bohlen and Burns, The Privilege to Protect Property by Dangerous Barriers and Mechanical Devices, 35 Yale L.J. 525, 528 (1926).

Each of the lawyers thus would appeal to a theory about the law's normative purposes and argue that the preferred principles and policies are better embedded in the legal experience. Moreover, by their citations, they would effectively argue that the favored purpose is better supported by the legal conventions. The defendant's theory calls attention to the wrongfulness of the plaintiff's conduct and requires no balancing of the interests at stake; by contrast, the plaintiff's theory calls attention to the value of human life and requires a balancing of interests. In retrospect, it should be apparent that the facts and legal experience presented above by the defendant fit well with the defendant's theory, as the facts and legal experience presented above by the plaintiff fit well with the plaintiff's theory. Each argument has a coherence of its own and integrates the facts in the trial record, the precedents on the books, and the principles and policies supported by the legal conventions.

From these sketches of arguments, it is not obvious how a court would or should decide this case: It is a harder case.[8] It is

---

[8] The decision of the Iowa Supreme Court on these facts is in Katko v. Briney, 183 N.W.2d 657 (Iowa 1971). The result is far less important for this discussion than the plausible legal reasons supporting each party.

possible, however, that full argumentation would show that one argument or the other can be accommodated more coherently with the facts, the legal experience, and the law's purposes. That is what the lawyers would seek to show in their full arguments. When judges decide harder cases, as suggested in Chapter 7, the lawyer who succeeds in presenting the more coherent argument—taking into account more of the relevant facts and the legal material—will make the more persuasive legal argument.

To review the preceding chapters in brief, the analogical and deductive forms of legal reasoning seem to promise clear and knowable answers to legal questions. This promise is seriously misleading. The unavoidable judgment of importance, resulting from the normative function of law and the family-style relations among cases, often precludes effective legal reasoning when it is confined to precedents and rules. Legal precedents do not themselves dictate the results in problem cases because each problem case differs from its precedents in some respects; to make a sound analogy, you must decide whether the differences between the cases are important enough to require different results. Legal rules do not dictate results because the language of a rule need only designate classes of cases; to reach a sound conclusion, you must decide which facts are important and justify placing a case in a legal class thus designated.

To make a judgment of importance, you may supplement the analogical and deductive forms with legal principles, policies, and professional conventions. Principles and policies provide accepted justifications for legal rules; you can use them to urge a judgment of importance that furthers the law's purposes. Legal conventions—the practices and dispositions of the members of the legal community regarding the lawful result in a case—support the principles and policies that are implemented in this way.

CHAPTER NINE

Legitimacy

LET US CONCLUDE BY reflecting from a different perspective on some implications of what we have studied. We have considered law and legal reasoning from the perspectives of law students, lawyers, and judges. We should not forget that the law affects other people, sometimes profoundly changing their lives in ways they do not welcome. This question may have occurred to you already: Why should the members of the legal community have so much to say about the legal reasoning in cases? Lawyers and judges are not elected and accountable democratically, with few exceptions. We surely have no credible claim to an inside line on truth and justice. Yet our interpretive role in law and legal reasoning gives us great power. Why should laypeople listen to an elite professional community and obey our prescriptions?[1]

The perspective of ordinary people calls into question the *political legitimacy* of the law and legal reasoning. In this chapter, I will cautiously suggest that the interpretive role of a properly constituted legal community is compatible with the legitimacy of the legal system in a democratic society like that in the United States. That is, ordinary people may have obligations to obey the law of a legal system in which interpretation depends on the conventions of a legal community. My purpose is not to pronounce whether the current practice is legitimate. It is to suggest a practical standard for gauging the legitimacy of the legal community's role and for reforming our practices to the extent they fall short. I hope you will consider my suggestions critically and continue to think about the problem of legitimacy as you learn more about the law and legal reasoning.

---

[1] See Paul Brest, Interpretation and Interest, 34 Stan. L. Rev. 765, 770-772 (1982); Sanford Levinson, Law as Literature, 60 Texas L. Rev. 373, 386 (1982).

A.   The Legal Conversation

Law and legal reasoning, as we have constructed it, is a matter of practice by a distinctive professional community. A *practice* exists when the members of a group generally conform their behavior to standards of conduct and think of conforming behavior as in some sense obligatory. Consequently, deviant behavior is criticized, and those who make such criticisms are not themselves criticized in turn. The standards then claim to prescribe what participants ought to do.[2] Generally, however, the standards do not claim to bind outsiders. Even among participants, dissenters may claim that they are not bound by what others think and do, however much the others may agree among themselves.

We can think of a practice as a (metaphorical) conversation.[3] Consider, preliminarily, a nonlegal example. A construction worker may have no difficulty whatsoever knowing what is meant by *straight line* when asked by a foreman to mark off the plan for a wall. A mathematician working with non-Euclidian geometries may find the concept *straight line* among the most troublesome. Only a pedant would challenge the construction worker's concept of *straight line* with the arguments of the mathematician. The lay notion is wholly adequate in the construction setting to accomplish the relevant purpose to the satisfaction of those concerned. It is as if the concept were used in a conversation, and the participants allow it to pass without objection. The worker, the foreman, the building contractor, the architect, the owner, and the city building inspector are the principal participants in the conversation. The mathematician is not a participant in that conversation. His objection is unwelcome and beside the point at hand.

Legal conversations, though more elaborate, have similarly distinctive participants and goals. Conversations about legal problems take place in courts, administrative agencies, the halls of Congress and the state legislatures, law offices, legal publications, the news media, and at the family dinner table. They usually concern concrete problems that require practical solutions. The

---

[2] This is adapted from H.L.A. Hart, The Concept of Law 55-61 (1961).

[3] The metaphor is adapted from Richard Rorty, Philosophy and the Mirror of Nature (1980) (without also accepting that there is nothing more to it than a conversation). See also Hans-George Gadamer, Truth and Method (1975).

participants vary with the problem. Notably, the conversation is influenced by people who are not present at the actual discussion. Substantially the same legal question moves from one setting to another before it is settled in one case. It arises repeatedly in a series of cases. What was said in a prior conversation, or is expected to be said in a future conversation, influences each actual discussion.

For example, a husband and wife, Richard and Lisa, may discuss a divorce. To trace out the implications for their family, they may mention what the family lawyer told one of them, or what they expect their lawyer to tell them, about the division of their property or child custody. They may go to their respective lawyers' offices to pursue the matter. What the two lawyers say in their offices will reflect what they have read in legal publications, including case reports expressing the views of the judges, statutes expressing the views of legislators, and scholarly works expressing the views of legal observers. The lawyers' contributions to the conversation will also reflect what they expect the local civil trial court to say if the parties seek a divorce. What the trial court will later say reflects what it expects the appellate court to say if an appeal were taken. What the appellate court will then say reflects what the judges have read in the relevant legal publications and the legal briefs of counsel, what the trial court said in its judgment in the case, and what the parties said to the trial court through their lawyers.

Metaphorically, a question concerning the implications of a divorce is the subject of a single, extended conversation that moves from setting to setting and, in sum, involves everyone who participates in the actual discussions. The dynamics of a participant's voice vary from one actual discussion to another: The appellate court's voice may be nearly inaudible at the dinner table, faint in the law office, stronger in the trial court, and dominant in the appellate court; Richard's and Lisa's voices may be dominant at the dinner table, strong at the law office, faint in the trial court, and nearly inaudible at the appellate court. But everyone who influences what course of action will be taken, as a consequence of the entire conversation, is a participant to some degree.

Individual cases are also part of a broader conversation about order and justice. The broader conversation extends through history with each case providing an occasion for it to continue.

Writings preserve the voices of the past; some judicial opinions from fifteenth-century England continue to affect legal problems in the United States, as do statutes from the middle ages and the writings of Roman jurists. Though a judge today would rarely read such materials in the original, the ideas they carry influence legal thinking today. Each judicial opinion concludes a phase of the legal conversation and makes a contribution that will be available in the next round.

The legal conversation shapes the participants' statements and actions as well as their very thoughts. Should Richard and Lisa seek a divorce, the legal conversation will determine how their property is divided and what kind of a relationship each may have with their children. Once Richard and Lisa enter the legal system, however, their voices grow faint as the lawyers take over. Clients commonly dread the loss of control they associate with seeing lawyers. Public anger at the legal profession partly reflects feelings of disempowerment commonly experienced by clients.

Assume that, in this story, Richard and Lisa get a divorce and a judge awards custody of the children to Richard alone. Assume further that Lisa is understandably outraged at the court's harsh judgment of her as a mother and also dreads the prospect of a distant relationship with her children. Her appeal fails, and she faces the question whether to run away with her children in defiance of the law. Morally speaking, it hardly suffices to tell Lisa that she should obey the law.[4] As the foregoing indicates, the law is, in important part, a product of an extended legal conversation to which she is an outsider. Moreover, the law that awards custody to Richard could be unjust, as Lisa no doubt believes. Or the law may have been just but was interpreted and applied unjustly, though in accordance with our legal conventions. What can we, participants in the legal conversation, say to outsiders who resist the changes we impose on their lives?

---

[4] Of course, it may be imprudent for Lisa to disobey because she will be caught and suffer. Let us assume further, however, that she just might get away with disobedience. The question for her then is a moral one: Whether she *should*.

B.   Legitimacy and Legal Reasoning

In general, legitimacy requires (1) that government action be lawful and also (2) that the law be justified as a matter of political morality. When these conditions are met, lay people are under moral obligations to obey the law. We then could say to Lisa that she should obey the law because it is right for her to do so. That may or may not matter to her; it should, however, matter to us. We should not want the law enforced unless enforcement would be legitimate.

The demand for legitimacy is central to the American political tradition, reflecting an historic commitment to individual liberty, human rights, and a democratic government of limited power. The concern is so central that it has a silent bearing on almost everything else in the law, shaping the legal conventions pervasively. Consequently, it is hard to master the basics of legal reasoning without appreciating the problem of legitimacy in the law.

Legitimacy requires the people who hold the reins of official coercive power to use it to implement the law—not arbitrarily, for their own benefit, or to oppress others. For example, the police are justified in using force, if necessary, to limit a person's freedom by lawful arrest if they have probable cause to believe that that person violated the law. The police are not authorized to arrest someone just because they do not like his attitude, disapprove of his life-style, believe him to be an immoral person, or oppose his group memberships or political views. As a matter of principle, all citizens are entitled to their liberty and dignity unless they violate the law.

Similarly, a judge issues or approves of orders backed by a threat of official coercion. When the judge awarded custody to Richard, he would have ordered Lisa to turn over the children. If Lisa defies the order, Richard can get a further order instructing the sheriff to take the children from Lisa and bring them to Richard. If Lisa persists in defiance, the sheriff then may seize the children forcibly. If she flees to another state, the sheriff there will do the same. The threat of enforcing judicial orders induces most losing parties to comply with court orders peaceably. Those who resist, however, will find themselves on the wrong end of a sheriff's revolver.

Anyone who stands before a judge, too, is entitled to liberty and dignity. We should want to know *by what right* a judge coerces other individuals (or approves of police conduct). Our tradition requires the judge to act for good and appropriate reasons—reasons that justify the implicit use of coercion. At the least, judges are under a duty to uphold the law and should act on legal reasons. Reasons of advantage to self, friends, or groups with which a judge identifies should be ruled out. Moral, religious, and political reasons should also be excluded unless they happen to be warranted by the law as grounds for judicial decisions. Judges decide within the law when they decide on legal reasons.[5]

Deciding within the law, however, does not suffice to achieve legitimacy. A precedent, rule, principle, or policy can be *legal* without being either just or required by political morality. Consider rules: Not all rules are legal in nature. There are rules of social etiquette, games, morals, scientific method, and other kinds. Most people probably think of rules as legal rules when they are in force in a society. Rules are in force when they are regularly applied by legal institutions (mainly courts) within a legal system that effectively guides the conduct of people to a large extent. In contrast, social rules, such as the rule requiring a man to remove his hat upon entering a church, some moral rules, like the golden rule, and other kinds of rules are not applied by legal institutions at all (or at least not regularly). These rules are not legal in character.

Rules need not be just in order to be legal. Until recently, for example, apartheid was the law in force in South Africa. You could determine what the laws of apartheid permitted and required by using legal reasoning. Assume, for example, that the manager of a municipal golf course denied entry to a black man solely because of his race. Under the laws of apartheid, the manager would be acting unjustly but lawfully. Under the Equal Protection Clause to the U.S. Constitution, by contrast, the manager would be acting unjustly *and* unlawfully. Legal reasoning does not operate differently in the two settings. It is used to identify and apply the law in force, for better or worse.

---

[5] Steven J. Burton, Judging in Good Faith (1992).

When so used, legal reasoning has practical, though limited, value. As Holmes put it:

> The reason why . . . people will pay lawyers to argue for them or to advise them, is that in societies like ours the command of the public force is intrusted to the judges in certain cases, and the whole power of the state will be put forth, if necessary, to carry out their judgments and decrees. People want to know under what circumstances and how far they will run the risk of coming against what is so much stronger than themselves, and hence it becomes a business to find out when this danger is to be feared.[6]

From a critical standpoint, moreover, legal reasoning can be used to identify objects for moral criticism. We can object to apartheid, rally others to protest it, and celebrate its demise, when we distinguish law from justice and morals. Legal reasoning, however, does not establish the justice or legitimacy of the law.

A law is just when it treats all people as they should be treated ideally—as God, who is infinitely just, would treat them.[7] The laws in force in any society fall short of perfect justice. There are three main reasons for this. The first is that we humans are fallible in its pursuit. Whether acting individually or in groups, governing by fiat or democratically, we make mistakes (and not infrequently). The second reason is that a system of perfect justice would not be administrable. Consider the age of maturity for purposes of voting. No matter what age is set, there will be individuals who, in justice, should be allowed to vote before that age and others who should not vote even later. An age is set, despite the over- and under-inclusiveness of the rule, for reasons of administrability, not justice. The third reason is that we need some way to impose a final settlement of disputes to short-circuit uncontrolled violence and to stabilize social intercourse. The law functions to settle disputes between people when they cannot do so on their own. For these reasons, the law in force in every society makes practical compromises with perfect justice.

---

[6] Oliver Wendell Holmes, Jr., The Path of the Law, 10 Harv. L. Rev. 457, 457 (1897).

[7] For a different view, see Ronald Dworkin, Law's Empire 165 (1986).

Political morality is not the same as law or justice. Political morality tells government to take its best shot at justice within practical constraints. It guides governmental action through principles of democracy, freedom of speech, equality, contract, property, due process, and other principles. It also tells government to modify the strict implications of these principles by considering human fallibility, administrability, and the need for finality. In addition, political morality indicates the political obligations of government's subjects, such as a citizen's obligations, if any, to obey the law. It tells citizens like Lisa, too, to take into account both justice and limiting practicalities. Few indeed would claim that government should not act, and that citizens are under no obligation to obey the law, unless and until the law achieves perfect justice.[8]

The problem of legitimacy arises within political morality so demarcated. Legitimacy does not signify that a precedent, rule, principle, policy or judicial decision is lawful. That depends on whether it is accepted as such by legal institutions within a legal

---

[8] To forestall misunderstanding, I consider political morality to be a part of critical morality, not conventional morality. Conventional morality contains principles that people in a community generally accept as guides to proper conduct. That one person or group *believes* a person's act to be wrong, however, is not a reason for that person to behave differently. For example, that Joan is outraged at Bill for working as an analyst for the CIA and believes that he should resign his job is not a reason for Bill to resign. Bill should do so if Joan is correct that the job is immoral or illegal. But Joan's feeling or belief then is superfluous because Bill should resign whether or not Joan is angry or believes that he should. We raise questions of legitimacy when we want to urge legislators and judges to behave differently, whether or not their behavior is popular. We can do that soundly with critical morality, which contains principles of proper conduct independent of anyone's beliefs.

Some people, of course, are skeptical of the reality of critical morality. Consider, however, whether you believe that slavery was wrong when and as practiced in the South in colonial times. Conventional morality cannot reach back and condemn it then, before much of anyone believed it wrong. The first abolitionist can argue that slavery is wrong only on the basis of critical morality. This is not to suggest, however, that we can know critical morality in any verifiable way. We can exercise our best judgment on the best available arguments, holding open at all times the possibility of error. See generally Michael S. Moore, Moral Reality Revisited, 90 Mich. L. Rev. 2424 (1992).

system that guides conduct effectively. Nor does legitimacy signify that a precedent, rule, principle, policy or judicial decision is just. That depends on whether it treats all people as they should be treated ideally, irrespective of human limitations. Rather, legitimacy signifies that government is acting as it should act, all things considered, including fallibility, administrability, and the need for finality.

When a law binds in political morality, people have (prima facie) moral obligations to obey. A law can bind in political morality in two main ways. First, it can be morally permitted and democratically enacted. Consider the laws requiring motorists to drive on the right side of the road. There is nothing morally objectionable about left- or right-sided driving; for the sake of safety and efficiency, it is morally desirable for everyone to drive on the same side. Morality permits the choice to be made by a majority. For these reasons, statutes requiring everyone to drive on the right side are justified in political morality.

Second, a law can be justified in political morality if, apart from democratic preferences, it would be morally right to enforce its obligations. Consider a law prohibiting everyone from torturing anyone. Such a law would implement a moral principle prohibiting anyone from intentionally inflicting unwarranted pain on another. It may be morally allowable for the state to enforce this moral obligation as a matter of law. The law would be justified by the same moral principle that binds the people to whom it applies. Consequently, a law prohibiting torture would be legitimate, even when a majority wants to torture a minority.

Our main focus, however, is on legitimacy and legal reasoning. In legal reasoning, the problem of legitimacy arises after we assume or conclude that the relevant laws are justified in political morality. The base points for reasoning by analogy and the major premises in deductive legal reasoning are then assumed to be morally acceptable (as well as legally valid). The problem of legitimacy arises if the results in cases do not flow from those starting points. This problem of legitimacy can be understood to arise in two ways.

Historically, the problem was conceived as one of constraining judicial decisions, one by one, in a formalist box. This could be done if legal reasoning allowed judges to transfer the legitimacy of a law to each judicial decision by applying the law to facts through a logically airtight chain of reasoning.[9] The law, together with the facts, then would fully determine the result in the case. There would be no room for a judge to decide on idiosyncratic reasons of advantage to self, friends, or groups with which the judge identifies, or on moral, religious, and political reasons when those reasons are outside the law. The judicial result would enjoy whatever legitimacy was enjoyed by the law.

We have seen, however, that such a formalist scheme is not ours in practice. Moreover, it probably could not be made to work in any society as complex as ours without abdicating important legal goals.[10] The judgment of importance is too often unavoidable; it breaks the chain of logic and blocks the transfer of legitimacy. We have not, however, concluded that the judgment of importance induces illegitimacy. To do so would be to accept the formalist criterion for legitimacy. Instead, we have suggested a kind of conventionalism. The problem of legitimacy arises here, too. But it takes on a markedly different cast.

On the conventional view, the logical gaps in a chain of reasoning are closed in accordance with the conventions of the legal community. We have already seen that, descriptively, these conventions guide and constrain judicial decisions.[11] Here, we consider normatively whether the conventions themselves, as the charge of a professional community with limited membership, contaminate the legitimacy of legal results in adjudication.

C.   The Legitimacy of Convention

By what right does the legal community play an interpretive role in legal reasoning and, therefore, in determining how the coercive powers of the state may be used? You might conclude that conventions of interpretation and judgment, shared among members of the legal community, are no better than a judge's idiosyncratic values. This conclusion, however, has profound implications for the current practice. It suggests, in particular, that we

---

[9] E.g., Duncan Kennedy, Legal Formality, 2 J. Leg. Stud. 351 (1973).
[10] See Chapters 2-4.
[11] See Chapters 5-7.

should do one of three things. First, we could maintain the demand for legitimacy and change our practices by radically restricting legal reasoning to stay within the formalist's box. This would leave many basic legal functions unperformed in our society. The laws of contracts and torts—and much else—depend extensively on standards of "reasonableness" that do not satisfy the formalist criterion for legitimacy. Second, we can give up the demand for legitimacy and continue current practices. This would be lamentable. The demand for legitimacy is central to the values at the founding of our democracy. Third, we can modify the demand for legitimacy so that our practices, or a moderate variant of them, can achieve legitimacy. We should not, of course, endorse a view of legitimacy just because it blesses the status quo. The whole point is to hold current practices up to a critical standard. We might, however, find that the traditional formalist view of legitimacy in legal reasoning was a bad idea all along.

In the remainder of this chapter, I will propose a response of the third kind. I will argue that a properly constituted legal community can contribute to the legitimacy of the legal system as a whole. When it does so, such a community enjoys legitimacy in its interpretive role. I will take a systemic approach.

1. Systemic Legitimacy

A systemic approach focuses less on the logic of legal reasoning in each case than on the benefits and burdens of a legal system and adjudicatory practices within that system. Think of the *legal system* as a coordinated set of legal precedents, rules, principles, and policies that guide the conduct of law-applying institutions, such as courts, and may be changed by lawmaking institutions, such as legislatures.

A legal system may offer considerable benefits to a society, including an end to self-help settlements of disputes with attendant risks of arbitrary violence, consistent implementation of principles and policies, and final settlements cutting off feuds and the like. A legal system can coordinate people's behavior in the interests of all, as by providing motor vehicle laws, commercial laws, property laws, and sundry other laws, often when it is more important that we all do the same thing than it is what we do. By prohibiting invidious discriminations, a legal system might foster a mutually respectful and cooperative community in which people might better flourish. Obviously, the benefits of a legal system can be substantial even when some of its laws fall short of justice or lack adequate justification in political morality.

Under a systemic approach, legitimacy is a property of the legal and political system as a whole, not an individual judicial result or a specific input into a decision. The judicial decision in a case, or the legal community's conventions, cannot be fairly appreciated in isolation from the institution of adjudication within a larger legal system. The legal system, in turn, is part of a political system that operates in a social, historical, and cultural context. Evaluating the legitimacy of legal reasoning in cases in isolation from the system, rather than the legitimacy of judicial practices in their full systemic contexts, is an academic exercise of little real concern to the people with interests at stake.

In a democratic society like ours, systemic legitimacy has two aspects. First, in its theoretical aspect, it requires that the people generally recognize an obligation to abide by the law, because it is the law. Whether the people generally recognize an obligation to obey the law is a factual question, requiring observation of attitudes and behavior in compliance with the laws of the system. Second, in its practical aspect, legitimacy requires that the legal and political system deserves allegiance from the people it governs. This is a question of political morality requiring normative evaluation of the system as a whole. (The old formalist view, by contrast, loses sight of legitimacy as the sign of an obligation to obey the law. It obsesses with the logical foundations of a judicial decision in place of the practical implications of that decision for people's actions.)

The theoretical question seems important for us because all theories of democratic government require the people's voluntary acceptance of the laws. Systemic legitimacy requires their acceptance of an obligation arising from the system, not their separate assent to each law or judicial decision. There is no law and no legal system, but instead anarchy, when each person picks and chooses the laws he or she will obey. We live in a diverse society in which we frequently disagree and in which few laws enjoy universal support. No individual can claim a right to disobey whenever he or she is convinced that a law is unjust, and grant others the same right, without in principle licensing disintegration of the entire system. So legal reasoning faces the tribunal of democracy, not on a case-by-case basis, but within a corpus of law and politics.

In theory, legal and political systems lack legitimacy when large numbers of people in fact cease to recognize an obligation to abide by laws or decisions with which they disagree, as in times of revolution, civil war, or civil disobedience. It is not easy to determine when the factual condition for legitimacy is met by an existing legal and political system, however. Whether people accept the legitimacy of the prevailing system depends on observations of social facts that would evidence recognition or rejection of an obligation to abide by the law.

The fact that most of the people comply with the law most of the time, for example, evidences their acceptance of such an obligation. It would be hard to imagine a people accepting such an obligation and, at the same time, generally disobeying the law. But the fact of widespread obedience is not dispositive of the theoretical question. Some people obey the law from a sense of obligation, others from a fear of sanctions for disobedience, and many from a combination of both motives. Obedience should not count as voluntary acceptance of the system when it is coerced by the state's threat of force. Indeed, it may only evidence the effectiveness of a police state. But how can one tell the extent to which obedience is not coerced? Many of us would be hard put to distinguish with confidence the roles of obligation and prudence or fear in our own law-abiding behavior.

There is also a good deal of disobedience to the law in the United States, as indicated by the crime rate and the huge number of people who are incarcerated. It seems far-fetched to interpret the disobedience of the typical mugger or tax cheater as a rejection of the legitimacy of the legal and political system as a whole. But identifying the disobedience that counts involves the observer in subjective judgments that may defeat the purpose of looking at the evidence. The observer's predispositions would seem inevitably to affect his or her interpretations.

In part because of these difficulties, the practical and normative question—whether the legal and political system deserves the allegiance of the people—is more important. The practical question for each individual guides his or her conduct. It precedes the behavior that makes up general obedience or disobedience to the law. Normatively, if you conclude that the system deserves respect, you probably should obey the law whether or not others generally do so. If you conclude that it does not deserve respect, you are not under an obligation to obey even if others generally do so. Therefore, people within the system who are concerned about legitimacy should conduct themselves so as to ensure that the system deserves respect.

Asserting that the American people should reject the legitimacy of their legal and political system is neither an idle act, a strong form of rhetoric to be used in political posturing, or an excuse for disobedience. Real claims of illegitimacy are fighting words. The American revolutionaries stood on a claim of the illegitimacy of continued rule by the British crown. Martin Luther King, Jr.'s defiant sit-ins were civil disobedience to illegitimate Jim Crow laws. Claims of illegitimacy may, of course, also extend to situations that are not so dramatically evidenced, such as the divorce of Lisa and Richard. Lisa's anger and disappointment, however, do not in themselves justify disobedience.

In my view, claims of illegitimacy are justifiably made when the legal and political system denies the most basic rights and interests of significant groups in society to a large extent and roads to changing the law within the system are substantially closed to those groups. The system must be so bad that compliance with wrong decisions is not justified by the benefits of the system as a whole. Recall the American revolutionaries' view of continued British rule and the civil rights movement's view of Jim Crow laws in the South. The claim, in each instance, was one of persistent oppression without hope of change through argument and lawful action within the system. The only alternatives were to submit to grave injustice or to resist. The oppressors, in each instance, were hard-pressed to say credibly that the oppressed group had an obligation to obey the law. To the oppressed group, the "law" was indistinguishable from domination by the powerful under a transparent cloak of legitimacy.

A crisis of legitimacy occurs when the legal and political system breaks down and tests of physical power replace legal and political argument. Crises of legitimacy can be avoided when the system respects the most basic rights and interests of all significant groups in the society and contains open avenues of legal change.

This permits each group to believe reasonably that it can change laws lacking a justification in political morality. A legal and political system that satisfies these conditions is engaged meaningfully in pursuit of a more orderly and just society with respect for all members of the body politic. Such a legal and political system has humility about its own fallibility. It welcomes criticism and proposals for legal reform from all members of the body politic. Even if we can imagine a better system, the venture may then deserve our respect as law.

Especially in a pluralistic society like that of the United States, all groups know that they will lose a few battles for laws they favor. Each will and should continue its participation in the system—turning away from disobedience—as long as it also wins a few and believes that it can win a few more. The U.S. system of government, if it stands for anything of constitutional dimension, should, in respect of all segments of society, be distinguishable from the British colonial rule against which the American revolutionaries acted.

The difference between systemic legitimacy and illegitimacy is one of degree in the extent to which a system treats all people fairly. The difference is not in the success or failure of a system to satisfy all demands—even all majoritarian demands—for reform. By contrast with the formalist view, systemic legitimacy is concerned with the conditions under which people have an obligation to obey the law. We should care whether the system, by comparison with alternative possibilities, treats all people fairly with an acceptable level of correctable error.

2.   The Legitimacy of the Legal Community

The preceding section suggests that a functioning legal system has value in political morality because it produces the benefits identified therein. This section suggests that a legal system cannot function unless supported by a legal or equivalent community that plays the interpretive role. If this is right, it would seem, a legal community has value in political morality when it supports a legal system that produces benefits for the population it governs.

Our historical, social, and cultural context includes three stable features that serve as appropriate starting points for this part of my argument: U.S. society is a large and complex society, a diverse society, and a society in which the people want the legal and political system to contribute to order and justice. These three facts suggest that a properly constituted legal community would play a legitimate interpretive role in that system.[12] Thus, I will argue: (1) the legal conversation focuses heavily on cases in a way that is distinctive and crucial in a large and complex society; (2) the legal conversation proceeds independently of majoritarian political processes so that minority rights might be protected by law; and (3) the legal conversation distinctively works out the implications of order and justice for the principles, policies, rules, and holdings in particular cases. Far from being a source of contamination, a legal community that serves these functions has value as a matter of political morality.

First, in a large and complex society like ours, it is not feasible for the broader society to make or pass judgment on each legal decision that must be taken. No one could read, for example, all of the appellate court decisions that are made every day, and those are only the uppermost tip of a gigantic iceberg. The society must delegate responsibility for operating and monitoring the legitimacy of the system in its details to a smaller group of people.

The people's elected representatives in Congress or the state legislatures are smaller groups. As members of the legal community, these representatives participate in the monitoring function. But they are too few to make and monitor the huge number of decisions taken each day. Legislators normally respond to decisions brought to their attention by constituents and lobbyists, and they monitor the judicial system from a political perspective that enhances its legitimacy. But, as an expression of presumably majoritarian or special interest preferences, they cannot establish

---

[12] The present membership of our legal community hardly reflects the diversity of the general population. Reasons of legitimacy support efforts to achieve a more diverse membership so that points of view otherwise likely to be neglected by privileged members of society can be better heard and taken into account by the law. This is needed, not to make the legal community democratically representative or to distribute law jobs fairly across groups, but to enhance the legitimacy of the legal conversation by hearing a wider range of arguments from previously inaudible voices. See David Millon, Objectivity and Democracy, 67 N.Y.U. L. Rev. 1 (1992).

legitimacy for the full range of cases. The legitimacy of judicial judgment is not a question of what a court can get away with in relation to majoritarian politics.

Lawyers and judges are society's experts on when—in what cases—the state may use its coercive powers legitimately. The legal community is, of course, a small part of the general population. It involves a larger number of people than could be elected feasibly. Most legal decisions are scrutinized by one or more lawyers for conformity with the law that provides for legal rights. Though lawyers are largely motivated to scrutinize decisions from the standpoint of their clients' interests, their goal is to protect their clients' rights. The case-orientation of the legal profession seems well-designed to monitor the legitimacy of a legal system in its details. Indeed, in any large and complex society concerned about law, some such professional community would be necessary to run and watch the legal system on a case-by-case basis.

Second, in a diverse society like ours, strictly majoritarian politics could hardly produce a legal and political system that satisfies the demand for legitimacy with respect to all significant subgroups. U.S. society is composed of many groups with differing perceptions, values, and interests. During long periods in American history, majorities have been able to enslave or oppress substantial racial, religious, ethnic, political, and other minorities. Systemic legitimacy requires that minorities, too, should accept the legitimacy of the legal and political system on the whole.

A professional community that operates at some distance from majoritarian politics is well positioned to maintain and enhance unpopular rights so that all people and groups in society are treated fairly. Adjudication provides an avenue of legal protection and legal change to everyone at individual initiative, regardless of political clout (though not, as presently constituted, regardless of financial ability). The legitimacy of the system would be enhanced if some such avenue were available to people who seek justice but may be unable to protect their most basic rights and interests through majoritarian politics. Adjudication, as part of a legal conversation about order and justice in cases, may offer a meaningful alternative to disobedience.

Third, in a society that is committed to order and justice, a legal conversation is a good idea. We should resist the temptation to equate majority preferences, or the preferences of any particular person or group, with the political morality that confers legitimacy. We know that majoritarian politics often are driven by passing cross-currents of public opinion or by coalitions of special interest groups; people's preferences often reflect personal experiences and values or narrow self-interest. We need not know what Order and Justice require, in a philosophically satisfactory way, to know that an orderly and just society would often be different from the preferences of people or groups. We may rightly believe that a legal conversation is more likely than other available alternatives to make a meaningful contribution toward that highly valued end.

An orderly and just society may encompass ample room for majoritarian or other political preferences to be heard and felt in the legal and political system. Yet it also may encompass room for a legal conversation using legal reasoning in a continuing effort to work out the implications of order and justice in cases. A professional community whose job is to worry about order and justice, as part of a larger system of law and politics, augments majoritarian politics so that the system as a whole includes the pursuit of a better society through law.[13]

In sum, a legal conversation can contribute to the legitimacy of the legal and political system because it serves these three functions within the system. The legal conversation focuses heavily on cases as needed in any large and complex society. It operates at a modest distance from majoritarian political processes so that minority rights might be protected. The legal conversation works out the implications of order and justice in cases. Consequently, legal reasoning is less influenced by political power or passing fads than by alternative ways of implementing the law's social vision.

At the same time, legal reasoning takes place in legal conversations that are distinctively professional. These conversations focus on what a court will or should do in a case. Judges are appointed by elected officials or elected themselves, and they generally must sign and publish their opinions to take public responsibility for those decisions. Judges do not decide what cases they shall decide, but must react to the initiatives of people who find themselves in

---

[13] To be sure, this role could be played by philosophers, economists, clergy, or laypeople. However, to the extent nonlawyers succeed in playing this role well, they will be transformed into the functional equivalent of a legal community, facing the same issue of legitimacy.

disputes. The judges must hear and respond to the arguments of the parties, who introduce the constraining conventions of the legal community through citations to the legal experience and the law's purposes. No one judge can make effective law without substantial support among many judges; any judicial decision is subject to overruling or subsequent neglect; and almost any legal question surfaces in a series of cases before different panels of judges. No group of judges can escape from the highly democratic checks of subsequent legislation or constitutional amendment and, ultimately, removal from the bench for misbehavior.

When thus placed in context, the legitimacy of a legal community's interpretive role seems plausible. The lack of an absolute assurance of legitimacy is troubling only when we accept the formalist idea of legitimacy in legal reasoning. Within the formalist view, judges and others will use any logical room in legal reasoning to decide on presumably improper grounds. If judicial decisions were a matter only of the judges' or the legal community's self-interest or political views, there would be every reason to confine adjudication to a far smaller scope than it has enjoyed.

The demand for legitimacy, however, is not a demand for consistent and complete logic in legal reasoning. Rather, it is a demand for limiting the use of official coercion to instances in which the state is enforcing its subjects' political obligations. Political obligations do not flow only by logic from rules implementing majoritarian preferences. They also flow from the practical advantages of having a legal system—even an imperfect one. To be sure, the benefits of a system are not always so great as to guarantee the system's legitimacy just because it is a system. In addition, it should have sufficient moral content to deserve respect commensurate with the demands it makes on its subjects. However, the systemic approach suggests that the interpretive role of a legal community can be legitimate in a context like that now prevailing in the United States.

I leave it to you to judge how well we are doing as you learn more about what we do. To the extent current practice falls short of full legitimacy, whether due to the legal community's composition, the law's current content, or other matters, we, the members of the legal community, should change it. The law schools are engaged in helping you spin a valuable web of beliefs about law. I hope that, if anything, this book has convinced you that a valuable web includes principles and policies, in addition to rules and precedents. I also hope that attention to principles and policies will open a door for you to criticize the prevailing law and proposals for legal reform on an ongoing basis. The legal community welcomes responsible criticism.

INDEX